Murders &
from
Yorkshire Dales

Peter N. Walker is the author of a number of highly successful thrillers. As Nicholas Rhea, he has written *Portrait of the North York Moors* in addition to the popular 'Constable' series.

He recently retired as an Inspector with the North Yorkshire Police to concentrate on his writing. He is married with four adult children and lives in Ampleforth.

Murders & Mysteries
from the
Yorkshire Dales

PETER N. WALKER

ROBERT HALE · LONDON

© *Peter N. Walker 1991*
First published in Great Britain 1991

ISBN 0 7090 4386 4

Robert Hale Limited
Clerkenwell House
Clerkenwell Green
London EC1R 0HT

Photoset in Palatino by
Derek Doyle & Associates, Mold, Clwyd.
Printed in Great Britain by
St Edmundsbury Press, Bury St Edmunds, Suffolk.
Bound by WBC Bookbinders Limited.

Contents

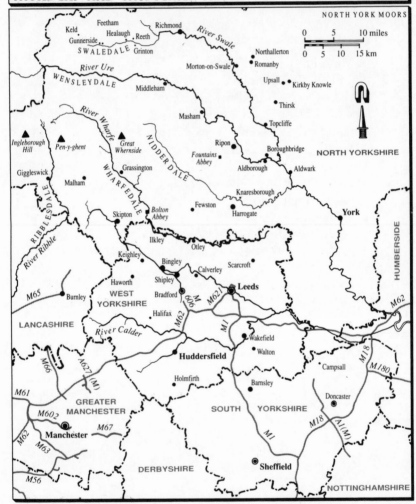

MURDERS AND MYSTERIES FROM THE YORKSHIRE DALES

NORTH YORK MOORS

0   5   10 miles
0 5 10   15 km

SWALEDALE

Keld
Feetham
Healaugh   Reeth
Gunnerside   Grinton
Richmond
River Swale

Northallerton
Romanby

Morton-on-Swale

WENSLEYDALE
River Ure

Middleham

Upsall
Kirkby Knowle

Thirsk

River Wharfe

Masham

Topcliffe

Ingleborough
Hill
Pen-y-ghent
Great
Whernside

NIDDERDALE

Ripon

Boroughbridge

NORTH YORKSHIRE

Giggleswick

Grassington

Fountains
Abbey

Aldborough
Aldwark

WHARFEDALE

Malham

Knaresborough

RIBBLESDALE

Skipton

Bolton
Abbey

Fewston

York

Harrogate

River Ribble

Ilkley

Otley

HUMBERSIDE

Keighley

Bingley

Calverley
Scarcroft

Haworth
Shipley

Leeds

Burnley

WEST
YORKSHIRE

Bradford
M606
M621

M62

LANCASHIRE

Halifax

M65

River Calder

M66

M627(M)

Wakefield
Walton

M62

Huddersfield

M180

M180

M61

Holmfirth

Campsall

M602

GREATER
MANCHESTER

Barnsley

Doncaster

M62
M63

Manchester

M67

SOUTH   YORKSHIRE

M18
A1(M)

M1

M56

DERBYSHIRE

Sheffield

NOTTINGHAMSHIRE

1   A Miscellany of Mysteries

The area known as the Yorkshire Dales is set in some of England's most impressive and unspoilt scenery. It stretches east from the mountainous Pennine fells towards the flat Vale of York and the dramatic coastline with its fishing villages and resorts. In so doing, it incorporates some of Britain's best-known villages, towns and cities which together boast a range of visitor attractions that are second-to-none. They range from the bygone charm and rustic atmosphere of Grassington to the bustle of Leeds, which is now a leading business and financial centre. There are country houses and parklands, waterfalls and caves, lakes and mountains, wild birds, plants and animals of enormous variety. There is the elegance of Harrogate, the contradictions of Knaresborough, the cobbles of Richmond, the architecture of Bradford and the cathedral of Ripon, plus the wonder of countless tiny communities that have for centuries endured a tough, open-air life on the steep and lofty fells.

It is an area of stunning natural beauty, with clean rivers flowing through broad and fertile dales. 'Dale' is the Norse word for valley, and above these green and pleasant stretches the fells rise in awesome and rugged splendour to be crowned by the famous Three Peaks – Whernside, Ingleborough and Penyghent. There are many smaller fells and hills, and many minor and remote dales as well as the large and famous ones such as Swaledale, Wensleydale, Nidderdale, Wharfedale, Airedale and Calderdale.

Each dale has its own natural and unique features which include local characteristics, differing dialects and the varied life-styles of the residents. In times past, few residents ventured from one dale to the next, for each dale was self-contained and separated from its neighbour by inhospitable countryside; now they are accessible to the world. They are rich in history and boast a remarkable collection of ruined castles, abbeys and historic houses. Many have been involved with the government of England since its earliest time and now provide the very stuff of legend and mystique.

The most westerly portion of the area lies within the Yorkshire Dales National Park, but beyond its boundaries are many other dales and countless places of interest, including some interesting Yorkshire towns and cities, both large and small. Every year, thousands of visitors arrive to swell the population to several times its normal size. They come to see the scenery and explore the towns and villages. Some hope to catch a glimpse of a way of life that seems a paradise compared with the daily routine of a suburban street or concrete tower block, while others come for the wildlife or the sheer joy of walking through magnificent countryside which is open, free and full of character.

Within such an area, there are many secrets and mysteries. Across the span of generations that are now part of the nation's history, many human beings have lived and died in this beautiful part of England, and so it has witnessed many stirring events. Some have formed part of our heritage, while others have been restricted to just one village or hamlet. In all cases, folk-memories tend to linger.

Over the centuries, this patch of England has seen much drama, sorrow and happiness. It has hosted births, marriages and deaths, but because the controlling force is human, these events have produced, or been the product of, anger, jealousy and revenge. As a consequence, and in spite of their peaceful external appearance or their ancient veneer of bucolic charm, the Dales have seen their share of mysteries and even murder.

This modest book does not seek to include every mystery or every unsolved crime or murder, but it does comprise a selection which might be of interest to those who wish to add a new dimension to their exploration of the intriguing broad acres of the Yorkshire Dales.

Ilkley's Swastika

Ilkley is famed as a spa town, once being known as 'the Malvern of the North' or 'the Heather Spa', due to its proximity to open moorland, but it is also known for its Yorkshire anthem.

This is the song which bears the title 'On Ilkley Moor bah't 'at'. In English, this means 'On Ilkley Moor without a hat', and it tells the sad story of someone who caught a cold and died through not wearing his hat while 'acourting Mary Jane'. We are not given a name for this victim of Yorkshire fresh air, but upon Ilkley Moor he died, was buried and was eaten by worms which in turn were eaten by ducks. Then 'we' killed the ducks to eat, and so, as the last verse says, 'Then we shall all have etten thee – on Ilkley Moor bah't 'at.'

Ilkley is a beautiful town with superb views across Wharfedale. It boasts wide streets and imposing buildings among delightful gardens and avenues of trees. With a history dating to Roman times, it later became the resort of those who sought better health through its clear and plentiful spa waters.

There are many walks around and above the town, one of which incorporates the curious Cow and Calf Rocks. On the face of the Cow Rock is the so-called footprint of the giant Rumbald who, while striding across the countryside from Great Almes Cliff, missed his footing and stood on the face of the Cow Rock instead of the summit.

To the south of the town, and lying behind it, is the moor which bears that giant's name – Rumbald's Moor, sometimes called Rombald's Moor or Rumbles Moor; it rises to over 1,300 feet.

A portion of this is the famous Ilkley Moor of the song, and upon these heights there are many rocks to explore, including the Panorama Rock with its extensive views. Some strange cup-and-ring stones are also to be found. These have also been discovered in Northumberland and Scotland and can be seen in other remote parts of the Pennine moors of North Yorkshire, especially above Nidderdale and Airedale. They consist of shallow hollows carved from the rocks, standing-stones or stone slabs; they are shaped like the bottom halves of cups and are sometimes surrounded by a ring also carved out of the stone; hence their name.

Several clusters of them are to be found around Ilkley and upon the nearby Baildon Moor and Snowden Moor. Among them, and a short distance to the west of the Panorama Stone, is what is thought to be the only Swastika Stone in Great Britain.

This is upon Woodhouse Crag and comprises a curious curved swastika which extends slightly more than a foot in width in each direction. This is thought to date at least a thousand years before the Roman occupation of Great Britain and, as with the cup-and-ring stones, its purpose continues to puzzle experts.

The giant arrows of Boroughbridge
Until the county boundary changes of 1974, Boroughbridge lay in the West Riding of Yorkshire, albeit on the boundary with the North Riding but separated from it by the River Ure. Today it is within North Yorkshire and is a pretty market town on the plain of York close to the meeting-point of two major rivers, the Ure and the Swale. Once a major coaching town on the Great North Road, it is now a pleasing and restful centre which

is an ideal base for touring the lower dales. The modern calm has occurred because Boroughbridge is bypassed by the A1 with its continuous roar of traffic.

Nearby is the village of Aldborough with its incredible Roman town of Isurium, and standing between Boroughbridge and the new A1 bypass is a row of three giant standing-stones. They can be seen only half a mile or so along the road to Roecliffe which leads from the Horsefair near the town centre; indeed, one of them stands almost on the verge of this minor road.

Known locally as 'the Devil's Arrows', they are three huge menhirs, megaliths or prehistoric standing-stones. Weathered by countless centuries of wind and rain, their heights are: northernmost – 16½ feet; middle – 21½ feet; southern – 22½ feet. Each is between eighteen and twenty-two feet in circumference. Fluted towards their summits, they stand in a long line running almost north–south very close to, and within sight of, the new A1; two are at one side of the Roecliffe road and one is at the other. In 1709 excavations were undertaken around the centre arrow to determine how deeply planted they were, and a report said,

A good soil was found about a foot deep, and then a course of stones, rough and of several kinds, but most were large pebbles laid in a bed of coarse grit and clay; and so four or five courses underneath one another around the pyramid [sic], in all probability to keep it upright, nevertheless, they all seem to incline a little towards the south-east. Under the stones was a very strong clay, so hard a spade could not affect it. This was near two yards deep from the surface of the earth, and a little lower was the bottom of the stone resting on the clay, and was flat. As much of the stone as was within ground, is a little thicker than what appears above, and has the marks of a first dressing upon it.

Until some three centuries ago, there used to be four standing-stones but one was demolished and smashed into small pieces to make materials for building a bridge across the local River Tutt.

There is a suggestion that several smaller stones stood within the group until Elizabethan times, when they were removed by the people of Boroughbridge who thought coins were concealed beneath them!

In common with so many other unexplained phenomena, the presence of these stones is accounted for in an old legend involving the Devil. In this case, he sought to destroy the Roman town of Isurium by firing his four giant arrows upon it. It is said he fired them from Howe Hill near Fountains Abbey and as they flew towards their target, he shouted:

Borobrigg keep out of the way
For Audboro town, I will ding down.

But every one of the arrows missed Aldborough (Isurium) and fell short, to become embedded in the earth in which they now stand.

Another theory is that they are Roman obelisks or even the boundaries of a Roman stadium or racecourse, and the sixteenth-century writer John Leland thought they were Roman trophies or obelisks which had been erected close to the Romans' route along Watling Street, here known as Deere Street. Yet another belief is that they once formed part of a huge druids' circle or even a square. Another authority believed they were ancient deities of the kind honoured by the Greeks and Phoenicians, who set up masses of standing-stones to honour their gods. But all these are speculation, and no positive answer has been provided.

What is known, however, is that the stone from which they are probably made is to be found some six or seven miles away, near Knaresborough, and it is almost certain that they came from there. The stone is millstone grit which is similar to that found in Cornwall, Dartmoor, Northumberland and Wales. Supplies of this stone are often close to the stone circles or burial-places of Stone Age people.

But even if the stones did come from nearby, how were such huge stones quarried and shaped, how were they transported and how did those primitive people manage to erect them? And why?

Aldwark's Conjuring Stone

Aldwark is a small village in the Vale of Mowbray, and it lies about six miles south-east of Easingwold.

Aldwark has a long and interesting history. In Roman times, a road ran this way from York, and a ferry was then used to cross the river; St Cuthbert is said to have travelled this way in the seventh century. In Saxon times the name meant 'old fort', the suggestion being that a Roman fort had been established here. In medieval times Aldwark lay within the huge Forest of Galtres, but even in Roman times the river was used commercially – landings were made near Aldwark; lead, minerals, farm produce, lime and coal were all conveyed by water to and from this village, even into this century.

Today there is no ferry across the River Ure, and instead the village boasts a toll bridge with many arches, some built of wood. There are two major buildings in Aldwark. One is the church built in 1846 in the shape of a cross, and the other is Aldwark Manor. The manor of Aldwark was mentioned in the Domesday survey, and it was inherited by the Fitzwilliam family, whose originator was a marshal in William the Conqueror's army. It came eventually into the hands of Lord Walsingham, and the fine house now serves as an hotel.

On the road beside the river, not far from Aldwark Manor, is a place called Hollow's Hole. This is said to be haunted, and nearby in Manor Wood is the curious Conjuring Stone.

The haunting and the stone are linked.

The stone is some two feet thick by four feet wide, and it protrudes from the ground for almost four feet. It lay hidden and forgotten until 1985, when it was rediscovered in its original position, albeit almost buried. It was uncovered and remains in its original location, which is on private property.

The stone bears some strange chisel marks. These may be due to ancient weathering, however, or even to the actions of glacier movements countless years ago, although some believe they resemble two faces. Whether they are the work of man or nature may never be known. How the stone came to be here is something of a mystery, although it appears that a glacier did carry it to this point. Its odd name is another puzzle, and there is a story surrounding the Conjuring Stone.

Years ago, a man is said to have committed many crimes in the area, and upon his death he was buried beneath this stone. Some stories say a witch is buried here, and an alternative name for the stone is Witches Stone. Others say the man was the witch, an odd claim, as most witches were female. Whatever the truth, or the sex of the buried person, its ghost restlessly walked the road nearby; this is the stretch known as Hollow's Hole. An old poem says:

Doomed for a certain time to walk the night,
And for the day confirmed to fast in fires,
Till the foul crimes done in his days of nature,
Were burned and purged away.

Fear of this ghost made the villagers uneasy and indeed frightened of travelling along this road at night, especially through the part known as Hollow's Hole. In the late nineteenth century it was decided to forgive the man his long-forgotten crimes and to exorcize his ghost. A priest, assisted by Mr Arthur Gray, President of the Cambridge

University Yorkshire Society and the Cambridge Antiqua-
rian Society as well as being a former under-sheriff of
Yorkshire, undertook this task. It was felt that, if the spirit
of this tortured witch was overtly forgiven and laid to rest,
the ghost would haunt no more. With due ceremonial and
ritual, the spirit was exorcized and laid to rest, and it was
'fastened down' with the Conjuring Stone.

Whether there are human remains beneath this stone
may never be known, but it has survived to remind us of
this odd story.

The Petrifying Well of Knaresborough

Knaresborough is a fascinating mixture of ancient cottages
and narrow streets, with a ruined castle perched above a
gorge through which flows the gentle River Nidd (see
Chapter 5). There is a commanding view of the river and
its famous bridge from the grounds of the castle, while a
short walk along the riverside is to be found one of
Knaresborough's most noted curiosities. This is the
mysterious Petrifying Well or Dropping Well. It has the
apparent magical ability to turn ordinary objects into
stone, and if anyone doubts this, proof is ever-present in
the array of petrified objects which are suspended in the
dripping waters.

A small stream flows through the woods above and
then drops over the cliff towards the river. But the steady
flow of mineral-enriched water has turned the cliff face
into a smooth yellowish apron of rock, and the waters do
not form a waterfall. Instead, they trickle gently
downwards, eventually to drip from the bottom of this
natural canopy. The build-up of sediment upon this rock
is so rapid that it has to be scraped clean every six weeks
to prevent its becoming top-heavy and collapsing into the
river.

All manner of things are suspended below, so that the
water drips constantly upon them – soft toys, stuffed
birds, gloves, hats, household items and personal

treasures. Depending upon the absorbency of the objects placed here, the transformation into stone can take between four and six months.

This is not a well in the accepted sense of the word, because visitors can stand upon the riverside footpath and contemplate the hardening objects which dangle above their heads. One does not have to peer into the depths to witness this.

As one looks upon these strange stone treasures, it is easy to understand how our ancestors thought these waters were magic. They firmly believed they could turn clothing into stone – and so they appear to do. When the traveller John Leland saw the well in 1540, he wrote of ' ... a Welle of a Wonderful nature caullid Droping Welle. For out of the great Rokkes by it distilleth Water continually into it ... what thing so ever ys caste in, or growith about the Rokke and is touched by this Water, growith into stone.'

But the power comes not from a magic potion but from the high level of rock-like calcareous deposits within the water. Very slowly, the dripping waters will transform into a stone-like texture the objects left there, and the visitor can inspect them in various stages of change. But it is a slow process, often taking months to transform some absorbent materials into a solid mass of limestone coating.

The Petrifying Well is upon private property, and a charge is made for admission; those who wish to turn their belongings into stone may do so for a small fee.

Even though we now know the secret of this well, it still presents an astonishing sight, and it is that much more mysterious because it lies very close to the cave of the Knaresborough witch and prophetess, Mother Shipton (for which an entry fee is also payable). Born in July 1488, she is reputed to have made accurate prophecies of developments such as the aircraft, although many of her so-called predictions are probably forgeries from a more recent time. A lot of them are thought to have appeared in the Victorian era, when some people were rather gullible. Many are undoubtedly the work of jokers, and some are known to have appeared after the events they purport to forecast. But not all Mother Shipton's prophecies were correct. She was wrong when she wrote:

> The world to an end shall come
> In Nineteen hundred and eighty one.

Masham's Druids' Circle

Situated in the lower reaches of Wensleydale, Masham (pronounced Massam) was once a thriving market town known especially for its sheep sales. Today it is a quiet place with a huge and practically deserted market square surrounded by interesting shops, houses and hotels. The church stands in one corner, its elegant fifteenth-century spire rising above the surrounding properties. Today the square is at peace in the winter months, but in summer it becomes one spacious car-park as visitors explore the alleys and shops.

There is little evidence of its former association with sheep sales, although sheep are still sold here in the autumn, albeit from the nearby auction mart. Some links with sheep do remain in a prize-winning breed known as the Masham. At its peak some 70,000 sheep were brought here from other dales, such as Swaledale and Nidderdale as well as other parts of Wensleydale, and they used the ancient drove roads as they were driven towards Masham for sale at the annual sheep fair each September.

The fair, which could trace its origins to a series of charters between 1250 and 1632, lasted two days and was the biggest sheep fair in the north of England. It ended shortly after the First World War, as increased mobility made other similar markets more viable.

One curiosity of Masham is the locally brewed and very strong beer known as 'Old Peculier' (spelt with an 'e'), named after an ancient ecclesiastical court which sat in

Masham and which was known as a peculier. One of the town's famous residents was Julius Caesar Ibbetson, a noted eighteenth-century landscape artist who is buried in the churchyard. Also in the churchyard is a strange pillar which may be part of a huge cross carved over a thousand years ago.

On the edge of the town is the beautiful Swinton Park, once the home of Lord Masham, a noted inventor and benefactor, and beyond the edge of this park, some three miles to the south-west of Masham, is the curious Druids' Circle.

Rather like a miniature Stonehenge, it stands at a location which is not easy to find: it is almost hidden among the conifers of Druids' Wood near the northern tip of Leighton Reservoir. The circle can be reached by road from either Masham or Healey; in either case, take the narrow, hilly lanes towards Ilton and look for the signs which indicate Druids' Wood. Some maps show this as Druids' Plantation. It is sometimes called Fairy Wood too, and contains a small car-park called Witches Car-Park. These all combine to provide a suitably mystic atmosphere, and the circle is a short walk through the trees. In winter, stout shoes or wellington boots may be necessary, due to the mud, but the trip is worth the small effort.

Upon seeing this magnificent but miniature Yorkshire Stonehenge in its hollow among the tree-covered hills, one could be forgiven for thinking it owes its origins to the druids and that it served some powerful magic or religious purpose in this remote and atmospheric spot, but in spite of its authentic appearance, it is a fake. The stones from which it is made might well be original and genuine stones from some long-abandoned stone circle of similar style, but this one was built around 1820. Designed by Mr P.T. Runton, it is roughly oval in shape and extends to about a hundred feet at the widest point. Two circles of standing-stones form the perimeter, one immediately within the other, and some of them are huge, rising to over ten feet in height with massive crosspieces.

There is an imposing entrance, and within the circle are a central phallic symbol, a flat sacrificial stone, a cavern which extends into the hillside behind to form a tomb, and other assorted standing-stones. There is also a chamber which might be the repose of a high priest, and some stone recesses which may have provided seating for priests or wardens of a lower rank. Or so it would all seem!

The impression that this is the haunt of bygone druids is enhanced by other constructions nearby. A walk around the circle will reveal several edifices of similar nature, and at the end of the footpath is yet another piece with long-distance views between the conifers and across Leighton Reservoir.

In all, this is a clever piece of work; some believe it is a genuine temple or druids' circle which has been transferred in its entirety to this place, while others know that it was built by a local benefactor for his own amusement and for the amazement of his friends and many guests.

The builder was the owner of Swinton Hall, Mr William Danby, who was a former high sheriff of Yorkshire. He lived at Swinton Hall in the early years of the nineteenth century and was the architect of wide-scale alterations to the house, so much so that the original almost vanished beneath his changes. When there was no work in the area, he gave employment to local men by creating jobs for them, even if it did involve the construction of what then appeared to be useless objects. Knowing that the local men were too proud ever to accept charity, he paid them good wages to build this Yorkshire Stonehenge. It was completed in the 1820s and became known locally as Danby's Folly. In addition to the bits and pieces in Druids' Wood, he constructed other follies, including a castellated bridge and a stone shelter with a seat overlooking the River Burn which he built in 1832 in thanksgiving for his rescue from pirates.

Access to the Druids' Circle is free and is by courtesy of both the Swinton Estate and the Forestry Commission, the latter leasing the land from the estate. Close to the car-park there is a picnic site, and the locality is wonderful for adventurous children – and their parents.

But in walking around this famous Druids' Circle, we must ask ourselves where these stones came from and where P.T. Runton obtained the design for William Danby. Is it a design he created or did he copy it from another such circle? Or was this entire circle occupying some other site before being transferred to Masham? Take a look and judge for yourself.

Some grave tales

From time to time in some of the Yorkshire Dales one comes across local names which reek of misery and death, such as the Valley of Desolation which, via a wooden bridge, leads off the Dales Way footpath near Bolton Abbey. I think it is named because a storm felled all its trees years ago!

On the North Yorkshire Moors there is the Lyke Wake Walk with its famous dirge, and high in Swaledale there was an ancient track known as 'the Corpse Way'. This was used by the upper dalesfolk to bury their dead, for the only church at which burials could take place was at Grinton near Reeth, lower down the dale. The Corpse Way followed a route from Kisdon Hill near Keld, crossed the River Swale and then roughly followed the route of the present road. It traverses the fellsides via Gunnerside, Feetham, Healaugh and Reeth to Grinton. For some mourners, the journey took at least two full days, for those in the higher reaches had to trek, with the corpse, for ten or twelve miles. Coffins were not used, because they were too heavy, the bodies being carried in lighter wicker baskets, and the work was shared between all the villages along the route.

Each village along the way loaned a couple of bearers so

that the journey was completed in a type of relay system. In these circumstances, it must have been very tempting at times not to bother with a formal funeral!

A similar trek was undertaken on the eastern slopes of the Vale of Mowbray. These hills form the western escarpment of the North York Moors. In about 1795 a certain funeral procession of the kind described above was wending its way from Upsall to Kirby Knowle, a journey of about one mile. The story is told by the Revd. A.J. Atwood, who was told it by one of the bearers, a lad of seventeen.

He and the other bearers were carrying a coffin containing the body of an elderly woman. It was a tiring task, for it was a very hot day in autumn. The bearers needed a rest, and they spotted some hazel nuts in Beckstead Wood. They would be a welcome refreshment, and so the men halted, placed the coffin on the ground and went into the wood to pick some nuts. When they returned and lifted the coffin onto their shoulders, they realized it was very much lighter. When they examined it, the coffin was empty. The corpse had vanished. There was no stream to wash it away, as the vicar was later to suggest, and no other explanation. They continued to Kirby Knowle with the empty coffin, and when they arrived at the church, they explained things to the vicar. No one could offer an explanation, and so the empty coffin was buried with due ceremonial, and it seems the relatives were none the wiser. The place where that coffin was placed while its bearers went to gather nuts is still known as Lost Corpse End.

Throughout Yorkshire there are instances of some rather odd graves and burials. While these are not mysteries in the full sense of the word, they are surely worthy of record in a book of this kind.

In the 1770s, for example, at Halifax, a woman was buried and the sexton was left with the job of filling her grave. But he was dishonest and before closing the coffin he had noticed the jewellery upon her fingers. With the intention of stealing her valuables, he left the grave open and returned at night specifically to remove the gems. He would then fill in the grave to bury the evidence of his crime. But as he lifted the lid of the coffin, the combination of fresh air and his attention to the rings on her fingers roused the lady in her grave! With a groan, she sat up and opened her eyes. He fled for his life as the risen lady marched home in her shroud to inform her astonished husband that she was alive and well.

In another instance near Halifax, Jonathan Walsh died in 1823. He owned Coldwell Hill Farm, and his will stipulated that he should be buried within one of his own fields. Furthermore, he had to be buried as far as possible from his wife, who was buried in the corner of another field.

Not far from Haworth, the home of the Brontë sisters, is The Old Gentleman's Grave. It is near the village of Oldfield, on whose outskirts is Oldfield Hall, sometimes known as Oldfield House. In 1835 a Mr James Mitchell was the owner and occupier of Oldfield Hall, and shortly before his death he instructed a servant to set a large boulder rolling down the sloping field. The rock came from the wall of his garden, and Mr Mitchell said that wherever the boulder came to rest would be his place of burial. And in 1835 Mr Mitchell died and his wish was carried out; he now lies peacefully beneath the trees and bushes in his former field.

Incidentally, apart from the family vaults of the Brontës, the churchyard at Haworth also contains the grave of Miss Lily Cove, Britain's first woman balloonist and parachutist. She was killed in a performance during an exhibition in 1906, when she became detached from her parachute and fell to her death. Her grave carries an illustration of a balloon.

A curious practice was undertaken by the Kitchenman family of Allerton Hall, Chapeltown, at Leeds. For more than 400 years every deceased member was carried from the house at night by the light of torches. They were then buried in the choir of St Peter's Church in Leeds. A massive chandelier with thirty-six branches was illuminated for the occasion, and the entire chamber draped with black velvet. Following the funeral, the family donated £50 to the poor of the parish.

At Kirby Malham in Airedale, the churchyard contains a tombstone through which a stream flows. The inscription has faded now, but it once said, 'As water parted us in life, so shall it in death.'

This was the grave of a sea captain and it seems that his wife was unhappy about his long absences at sea. When he died, she said that, because water had separated them for so long during life, it should continue to do so during death. She wanted her grave to be at one side of the stream and her husband's on the other, but when she died, the rock beneath made it impossible to excavate her grave. The sexton had to place her coffin on top of that of her husband, and so her wish was never fulfilled. But water now flows over both and no longer separates them; in fact, it united them.

At Richmond in Swaledale, Robert Willance was riding home and had an accident which resulted in the amputation of his leg. It was buried in the churchyard, and when Willance died later, he joined his leg.

Even more curious circumstances surrounded Pie Leach's grave at Keighley. James Leach was known as 'Pie' because he sold meat pies around the town, and it seems he was something of a local character. He hit upon the idea of providing his own grave well before his death, and so he had his grave excavated and also ordered his coffin. Even his tombstone was erected in 1887, six years before his death. But the undertaker was unhappy about the unknown length of time before the real funeral, because of storage problems for the coffin and, of course, his fees. Pie hit upon a simple solution. The coffin would be stored in the grave, and so the usual fees for opening and closing the grave could be paid.

Pie Leach finally joined his coffin on 13 October 1893.

Yet another curious grave is in the churchyard at Rossington, near Doncaster, although its precise location is unknown. It is that of the King of Gypsies, Charles Bosville, who died in 1708. After his death, it was the custom of the gypsies to visit his grave once a year and to pour over it a flagon of beer.

At Rawcliffe on the River Aire, a local celebrity had a bizarre idea for his funeral; he was ninety when he died and insisted that his coffin be carried by twelve old ladies to the music of a Yorkshire fiddler and a Scotsman on the bagpipes.

If there is any element of mystery behind these strange events, it is quite simple – what makes people behave in such peculiar ways and why do people desire such a strange exit from the world? Perhaps it is to keep their names and deeds known to the countless generations yet to follow.

In that, many have succeeded.

2 Tom Lee of Grassington

Grassington is variously described as a small town or a large village, but few dispute that it is one of the most charming of the communities to be found in the Yorkshire Dales. With its cobbled streets, pretty stone houses and beautiful setting in Wharfedale, it is now a magnet for tourists. It is the location of the Yorkshire Dales National Park offices and other agencies such as the Upper Wharfedale Folk Museum and a mountain rescue post.

In spite of its charms, however, there is a dark side, for folk-memories still recall the crimes of Tom Lee, once a blacksmith in the village. His old smiddy, the local name for the blacksmith's shop, is still pointed out, and it can be seen in the main street, where it bears a plaque which declares its place in Yorkshire's criminal history. Lee earned the unenviable reputation of having three charges of murder levelled against him – and all in respect of the same victim. Two of the charges were not proceeded with, due to a lack of evidence, but thanks to a twinge of conscience by a brave witness, the third charge did result in his trial at York Assizes.

Grassington was once known as 'Girston', and in Lee's time the surrounding hills were busy with lead-mining enterprises.

There was plenty of work for a skilled blacksmith, and good money could be made, but Grassington's blacksmith did not relish hard work. He liked to spend money but did not like to earn it. His name was Tom Lee, and he was a strong young man in his late twenties with the powerful physique of his profession. He was also very hot-tempered and quick to anger at the slightest hint of trouble; he could erupt from a calm, rational man into a fierce, fighting maniac in a matter of seconds. It is true that the villagers were frightened of him, and few of them would dare to cross him; in short, Tom Lee was dangerous and he was a bully.

If he was short of money, his work, if properly conducted, should have brought in sufficient for his needs, because he was also landlord of the Blue Anchor Inn. This was run largely by his wife. It seems that his financial worries were known to the local people, because when several burglaries and housebreakings occurred in the area, along with thefts of cash and other petty objects, it was Tom Lee who fell under immediate suspicion. There was never enough evidence to bring a charge against him, however, on top of which none of the villagers dared to become a witness against him. If anyone testified against him, and the case failed, the life of that person would not be worth living. So the people of Grassington maintained a discreet silence about the identity of the criminal who lived and worked within their midst.

At that time, Grassington was the lead-mining capital of this dale; the mines were on the moor and belonged to the Duke of Devonshire. They produced about 700 tons per year. Two hundred men were employed, and one of the pits was over a hundred fathoms deep, a fathom being six feet in modern terms. The wages for these men were brought by a man called 'the running postman', a powerful man who might one day have to defend the money against highway robbers. He carried a pistol for this very purpose. His job was to carry the money to the counting-house for distribution to the men. The counting-house was at Yarnbury, just over a mile and a half from Grassington along Moor Lane, and the former buildings of the mining enterprise can still be seen, along with areas of disused mines and pit shafts.

Tom Lee, desperately in need of money, knew the route and movements of this man and decided he would relieve him of his cash. In heavy disguise as a highwayman and mounted on a horse, he lay in wait on Moor Lane just outside Grassington. Sure enough, the postman rode towards him. But the man was not to be easily robbed. He kicked his own horse into a gallop and decided to outrun the highwayman. But Lee gave chase and overtook him; Lee had a huge club, and he began to thrash the galloping money-man with it, at the same time trying to grab the bag of cash he was carrying. But the money-man drew a pistol and managed to release a lucky shot at Lee. It hit him in the shoulder and threw him from his horse.

It was not a fatal wound, but it was nasty, and it was bleeding severely. Lee had to give up that attempt but now had the problem of the serious wound, for it would surely lead to his identification if the postman lodged a complaint. Some accounts say that the postman did not fire any shot but simply gave Lee the thrashing of a lifetime. That thrashing was enough for Lee to require medical attention by a doctor. Whatever did happen to Lee, it taught this bully a lesson: it halted that robbery.

Lee managed to reach a quiet place where he hid all day and all night, but his condition was such that he required urgent care. He knew there was no alternative, and so he crept back into Grassington under cover of darkness by using one of the many footpaths in that area, and knocked on the door of Dr Petty.

Petty gave him treatment, but the story of the abortive robbery had already circulated the village, and Dr Petty realized that Lee was the culprit. He gave Lee every possible assistance for his wound but for some reason did not inform the authorities of his knowledge. It was to prove a fatal lapse, but he respected the confidentiality that exists between doctor and patient. It seems that the doctor was one of the few people who were not afraid of young Lee. Dr Petty was bluff, happy and highly respected in and around Grassington, well liked by everyone, and he was one of the few people brave enough to risk straight talk to Tom Lee.

'Look, Tom,' he said, 'I know you are guilty of that crime but I'll respect this confidentiality because you are my patient. But mend your ways, because if you do get caught, you'll go to the gallows.'

It was good, fatherly advice to an errant young man, for the crime of highway robbery then carried the death penalty, and it seems that, for a few months, Lee did behave himself. The incidence of thefts and housebreakings was reduced and the villagers reckoned that Tom had changed for the better, because he could be seen earnestly working in his smithy; he even employed an apprentice.

For a while, therefore, an uneasy peace settled upon Grassington; whether it was through Lee's fear of Dr Petty's knowledge, or possibly fear of the money-carrier, we shall never know. But a strange event brought matters to a brutal climax.

It seems that underneath his 'new' exterior, Tom Lee did nurse a smouldering hatred for Dr Petty, perhaps fuelled by the knowledge that one word from Petty could dispatch him to the gallows. That hatred was to grow into a mania. But the doctor had other things to concern him; in his view, his words to Tom had been heeded. His practice covered a huge area of the Dales, including the villages of Conistone and Kilnsey, higher in Wharfedale. These communities are situated on opposite banks of the Wharfe, separated only by the river.

Dr Petty travelled by horse to visit his patients but some of the roads were dangerous, some ran by the side of the river, and others crossed dark and frightening woodland. One such woodland was Grass Wood, which even today is midway between Grassington and Conistone. The route from Grassington is called Grass Wood Lane. The route from Kilnsey continues to pass through that wood if one travels via Conistone from Kilnsey to Grassington along the east bank of the Wharfe, and several footpaths also traverse the wooded area.

One day in October 1766 Dr Petty was visiting patients at Kilnsey, which is famous for its massive overhanging rock known as Kilnsey Crag. By chance, Lee was also in the village. He was drinking in the Anglers Arms, the local inn. During the late afternoon or early evening, Dr Petty chanced to be walking past the inn when he became aware of a fairly boisterous disturbance inside. This was an argument between Tom Lee and his companion, a young farmer called Dick Linton. They were together in the parlour, and it seems they had consumed a considerable quantity of ale, because Linton started to suggest that Lee was the person responsible for many of the local crimes. Lee defended himself, knowing the dire risks of being identified. As the discussion became more heated, it developed into a shouting-match with curses and threats, and it was clear that a physical battle was about to commence. Each man was powerful and angry; it would have been a memorable contest, with flailing fists and much bloodshed.

It was at that crucial stage that Dr Petty walked into the inn to savour a meal accompanied by a glass of wine and a smoke before returning to Grassington. He saw Tom and, in his firm, no-nonsense manner, asked what the commotion was about. Linton, his courage aided by the drink, blurted out that he was sure that Lee was a criminal, but Dr Petty saved the day by telling Linton to be quiet. Then he turned to Tom and reminded him of that earlier meeting, adding that if Tom did not mend his ways, he would surely end his life on the gallows. As a form of threat, he reminded Lee that he knew more than most other people about some aspects of Lee's recent past.

Instead of regarding the doctor as an ally and friendly adviser, Lee saw him as a threat, an enemy; this chat strengthened Lee's view that Petty was the one person who could send him to the gallows. Lee fell into a moody silence, sullen and full of smouldering anger as he finished his drink. Then, as the inn filled with local people, he slipped away, and his absence was barely noticed by the others. Later it was time for the doctor to leave, and such was his popularity that the landlady followed him out to his horse. Someone brought it to the door of the inn and he mounted, making sure he had all his equipment, his bag, his coat and hat and other necessities for the long, cold ride back to Grassington. He had one more call before reaching home.

As he mounted the horse, he noticed the landlady was carrying the traditional farewell glass of hot whisky, a stirrup-cup. (It was customary to give departing guests a stirrup-cup when their feet were in the stirrups ready for moving off). The drink was contained in a glass, and the landlady passed it up to him. He took it and drank the contents, then passed it back to the lady. In the heat of the moment, the glass slipped from his grasp and fell to the ground – but the glass did not break. It rolled to safety near the door. There were gasps of horror from the assembled people, and even Dr Petty turned pale at this occurrence, because, according to a Dales superstition, to drop a stirrup-cup glass and to have it unbroken as a result was an omen of death. Some saw this as a clear warning for the doctor, and the terrified landlady pleaded with him not to ride home that night, suggesting he remain at the inn. But he refused. He had more work awaiting and he wanted to get home to be with his wife beside his own roaring log fire. In any case, the doctor was not a man to take heed of ancient superstitions. So he spurred his horse into action and left the Anglers Arms.

His route took him along the high track from Kilnsey via Conistone village, where he tended a patient, and then he rode on through Grass Wood. In fact, there is still a high route from Conistone which leads across Little Lathe via Lea Green to link with the Dales Way long-distance footpath before reaching Grassington. This route passes the top of the modern Grass Wood above the adjoining Bastow Wood, and there are other paths, any one of which Dr Petty might have used.

But Tom Lee knew which of these routes would be taken by the home-going doctor, and he lay in wait behind a drystone wall as darkness enveloped the woodland. As the doctor's mare trotted happily through the wood at a point known as Dibb Scar Glen near the northern edge of the wood close to Dibb Beck, a figure rose from the side of the track. The man seized the reins with one hand, and with the other dragged the startled doctor to the ground. So sudden and unexpected was the attack that Dr Petty had no chance to defend himself, and as he lay winded on the ground, he was savagely attacked.

Some reports say a pocket knife was used, and others say that the weapon was a cudgel. Although the tough doctor fought back with all his power and strength, he was battered into unconsciousness. There was a lot of blood, and the awful noise of his terrified shouting frightened his horse. It galloped off, and his assailant, believing he had killed the doctor, dragged the body into the undergrowth and concealed it among some rocks, then covered it with vegetation. Knowing that the horse would alert the villagers to the fate of the doctor, the assailant then ran off and made for home.

The attacker was, of course, Tom Lee. He returned to his home in Grassington, covered in blood and in a state of high excitement. It was late and very dark when he arrived, his clothing torn and smothered with blood. His face was covered in bruises, for the tough doctor had given a spirited defence of his life.

It was clear that he had been involved in some awful adventure. His wife, quite tolerant of his late-night excursions and unlawful behaviour, realized that that night's adventure had been out of the ordinary and began to quiz him about his state. At first Lee refused to tell her what had happened, but eventually he admitted his guilt. It seems that he did this because he needed help to move the body of the doctor to a more secluded hiding-place and because he knew that, in law, a wife could not testify against her husband, so he had decided she was the person to assist him. By doing so, she would become an accomplice, and this, he reckoned, would compel her to keep his secret.

But as they discussed the best method of achieving that purpose, they realized they would probably need someone with more strength than she could muster. The name of Lee's apprentice was mentioned and then, with horror, the couple realized that he, a youth called Bowness, might well have overheard their conversation. The first minutes of Mrs Lee's inquisition had been loud and angry. Bowness occupied a room next door, separated only by thin walls.

Lee went to the lad's room. When he entered, Bowness cowered on his bed, quaking with fear, and admitted he had heard everything. He offered to take an oath of silence, but Lee had another means of ensuring his silence and his co-operation. Instead of his wife, he would enlist the lad's help to move the body and thus make him the accomplice. That would guarantee his silence. Bowness, terrified beyond all measure, promptly agreed.

And so, in the early hours of that same morning, the two men entered the wood under cover of darkness to carry out their deed. They carried a large sack, and their plan was to move the body to a peat bog on the moors and there to bury it. But when they arrived at Dibb Scar Glen, Lee was horrified to find the doctor still alive. He was crawling about in the darkness with his awful injuries, shouting for help. So Lee was faced with another problem. He solved it by making sure the doctor was dead.

With his unwilling accomplice, he battered the poor doctor with a length of a stout branch until he was sure the man was dead. He then threatened Bowness with a similar fate if he did not assist him with the removal of the body, and so they dragged it through the woods and onto the moor. There they buried the still-warm body in a peat bog. It was wrapped in the sack. Having achieved this, they returned to the smithy at Grassington to await developments.

That morning, when the doctor's mare arrived home riderless, there was immediate concern. The horse was covered in dirt, its reins were broken and his bag was still fastened to the saddle. But of the doctor there was no sign and no word. A search was organized, and although signs of a struggle were found in Grass Wood, no sign of the doctor was found.

Enquiries were made in all the villages which Dr Petty had visited, and news of Lee's confrontation with Dr Petty in the Anglers' Arms at Kilnsey did reach the ears of the people of Grassington. No one voiced any suspicion, but they guessed the truth. The urgent whisperings among the villagers left Lee in no doubt that everyone knew of his guilt, even if it could not be proved. Then Bowness, his unwilling assistant, decided he could not tolerate working with Lee and left to find work elsewhere. Eventually he obtained a post in Durham.

Amid the speculation that was circulating Grassington, it reached Lee's ears that peat had wonderful powers to preserve human remains. The people said that, when a corpse was buried in peat, it did not decay as it would if buried in soil; it had an embalming effect, so that a body could remain in a good condition and continue to be identifiable for years and years. Then an old farmer recalled having seen Lee at the dead of night on the peat moor above Grass Wood ...

All these factors filtered back to Lee, and they began to prey on his mind. He knew that, if the rumours persisted, someone would search the peat moor. It would be a massive task but there might be indications of recent activity where he had buried the doctor. He felt sure that the body would be discovered, and decided he must move it again. Some accounts suggest it was moved from one peat grave to another, but there was certainly one change of venue for the doctor's grave. On that occasion, Lee enlisted the help of his wife and the services of a pony.

It was now several weeks after the doctor's disappearance, and the speculation had dwindled somewhat as Lee and his wife set out, under cover of darkness, to go about yet another grisly task. They exhumed the body still in its sack, placed it on the back of the pony and carried it across the moors towards Grassington. They used a network of footpaths, some of which still exist, to trek to the east of Grassington towards Hebden and eventually reached a point above the River Wharfe between Hebden and Burnsall. That terrible trek would be around three miles in extent, and it ended at a place called Loup Scar near Burnsall. (The road leading past this is still called Skull Road; Loup Scar overlooks the River Wharfe on the north bank. On the south bank of the river, the Dales Way footpath passes this point.) Here the body was taken from the pony, weighted with a large stone and thrown from the north bank into the River Wharfe.

But the fates were not on the side of Tom Lee. It was now Sunday morning, and a man was making his way home along that footpath, having spent the Saturday night courting his girlfriend at Burnsall. In the early hours of that morning, he heard the noises of their movements and concealed himself to watch.

In the dim light of early morning, he saw a man and a woman cast a large, weighted object into the river, and he heard the splash as it entered the water. It sank immediately and remained in position, due to the heavy rock which acted as an anchor. The man and woman then left the scene with a pony. The witness decided that whatever had been dumped was probably the result of something illegal, and he informed the authorities.

Mindful of the continuing mystery of Dr Petty's

disappearance, a search of the river at Loup Scar was quickly arranged. The body was recovered where it had been thrown in, thanks to the rock-anchor, and it was immediately identified as that of Dr Petty. The injuries to the corpse left no doubt that he had been the victim of a savage killing.

The news quickly spread throughout the dale, and the vicar of Linton, the Revd Alcock, halted his morning service to announce the discovery to his congregation. As there is no parish church at Grassington, services are held at Linton, and so this was the doctor's local church. In this way the people were formally told of the awful fate of their beloved doctor.

An inquest was quickly held at the Bridge Tavern, and the sad remains of Dr Petty were buried.

Tom Lee was still the chief suspect, but he rested in the knowledge that a wife could not, in law, testify against her husband. There is little doubt that he felt secure, for there was no proof or evidence that he had been concerned in the death of Dr Petty. There was a lot of rumour and speculation about his guilt, but no hard evidence, and Bowness was now working many miles to the north.

Lee's contentment was short-lived, because he was taken into custody on suspicion of murdering Dr Petty. But the magistrate found there was a lack of evidence and dismissed the charge. Lee was now in a celebratory mood, but it lasted only a few minutes because, as he walked away from that hearing, a constable was waiting outside. He produced a warrant signed by a Skipton magistrate, Mr Tobias Sedgwick, and so Lee was again taken into custody. The following day he appeared before the magistrates on a charge of murder. This time the court appeared to believe there was some substance to the charge, and Lee was remanded in custody for a week while further enquiries were made. At the end of that week, he appeared before the magistrates, but there was still a lack of firm evidence against him, and he was freed.

The court felt there was insufficient evidence for a charge of murder to be sustained at the next assizes.

In these two cases, neither was a criminal trial; these were preliminary hearings known as committal proceedings. Their purpose was to examine the available evidence to determine whether or not a suspected person should be committed for trial at the next quarter sessions or assizes. In both cases, the magistrates decided there was insufficient evidence, and so Lee never stood trial. Contrary to some reports, he was never found 'not guilty' and acquitted – if he had been, he could not have been retried for the same crime. He was twice charged with murder, but neither charge was sustained.

With two such hearings behind him, it now seemed that Tom Lee had beaten the judicial system, and he returned to a normal life in Grassington. There is little doubt that the people did their best to ignore him and to express their revulsion at his criminal character, but we are not told whether he resumed his criminal career. It is possible that he did recommence his housebreaking and thieving, probably feeling that he was immune from prosecution, but he was not a welcome member of the community at Grassington.

Yet the story does not end there. Three years later young Bowness, Lee's former apprentice, was still working in Durham, and his conscience bothered him so much that he went to his employer to discuss his role in the murder of Dr Petty. His boss listened carefully and then summoned a magistrate. Bowness told his story, on oath, before this magistrate, and thus the legal processes began anew. This time there was some firm evidence to link Lee with the murder of Dr Petty, and he was again taken into custody. At this most recent committal proceedings, the magistrate did feel there was sufficient evidence to justify a hearing at York Assizes, and so Tom Lee was committed to York Castle to await his trial.

The evidence of his former apprentice was sufficient for

the jury to return a verdict of 'Guilty', and so Tom Lee, the violent Grassington blacksmith, was sentenced to death. It was a fate which had been predicted by his victim. He was hanged on York's Knavesmire on 25 July 1768, and afterwards his body was taken to Grassington to hang in chains from a tree in Grass Wood. The place became known as Gibbett Hill, and for years afterwards the people of Upper Wharfedale referred to it as 'Dark Corner'. It is said that eventually the irons fell away from the tree and became buried somewhere on Gibbett Hill. Lee's remains hung there for a long time, and for some years there were stories of ghostly hauntings, frenzied hoofbeats and weird screams in that wood.

Today Grass Wood is on the tourist trail, for it offers beautiful views of Wharfedale, but it will be a long time before its links with the notorious Tom Lee are forgotten.

3   Kirklees –
The Burial-place of Robin Hood?

Was England's most famous and best-loved outlaw, Robin Hood, murdered in the Yorkshire Dales by a jealous cousin, or was his death at Kirklees Priory an unfortunate accident? In speculating upon this matter, it is also interesting to examine evidence which might determine whether or not he was a Yorkshireman rather than a man of Nottingham. Certainly there is reason for believing that many of his exploits occurred in Yorkshire and that Nottinghamshire and Sherwood Forest were not his main haunts. That he died at Kirklees Priory in Yorkshire is well documented in accounts of his life.

Today the name of Kirklees frequently appears in association with the Kirklees Metropolitan Council, the West Yorkshire local authority whose head office is in the town hall at Huddersfield. The council's boundaries embrace a considerable area of urban West Yorkshire and include such well-known places as Huddersfield, Dewsbury, Batley, Cleckheaton, Heckmondwike and Holmfirth. The latter is known as the setting for the BBC television series *Last of the Summer Wine*.

The modern and sprawling Kirklees bears little or no resemblance to the tiny ancient place which provided the name for this modern local authority.

The original hamlet is difficult to find unless one knows the area very well, a fact which is odd bearing in mind that Kirklees is the reputed scene of Robin Hood's death and burial. The ancient Kirklees, which was situated in the rural splendour of beautiful Calderdale between the River Calder and Hartshead, may be difficult to locate upon a fairly modern map simply because it has been surrounded by urban and industrial development. Furthermore, the site of Robin Hood's grave and the building in which he is reputed to have died are both on very private premises which are not open to the public.

Nonetheless, Kirklees has a considerable history. Within Kirklees Park are the remains of a small Roman fort which was part of a network of local defences, but by the time of William the Conqueror the area was wasteland. Later, in 1155, a priory of Cistercian nuns was founded at Kirklees by Regner de Fleming, but after the priory fell into ruin, many of its stones were used in the construction of Kirklees Hall.

This impressive house was built in the reign of James VI and I (1566–1625) and became the seat of Sir George Armitage, whose descendants still own the land. Today it stands in a park of 170 acres with beautiful gardens, a lake, a stream and some fine specimens of beeches, oaks and chestnuts. During the last century it was described as 'large and well-timbered, full of sunny glades and speckled with the black shadows of immemorial yew trees'.

In spite of so much of the priory's stone being used to build the Hall, many portions of the original church did survive. A buttress and two piers of the north nave remained to identify the site of the old church, as well as part of the prioress's lodgings. The beautiful gatehouse remains, with its timbered gables, three storeys, small windows, stone steps outside and a carved beam bearing carvings of four dogs.

The countryside surrounding this old ruin was featured by Charlotte Brontë in her novel *Shirley*: the Hall is said to be 'Nunneley' and the park became 'Nunwood'. Charlotte's knowledge of Kirklees resulted from an extended visit to the district. On 19 January 1831, as a schoolgirl, she came to stay at Roe Head, a pleasant house just above Kirklees Park, and she remained there for eighteen months. She learned a lot about local history, including the events of 1812 when working people revolted against the introduction of machinery. Her time at Roe Head, and the friends she made in this area, had an undoubted influence upon her future writing career.

But by far the most famous person to be associated with Kirklees Priory is Robin Hood, and it is the long-surviving gatehouse which has earned itself a place in the folklore surrounding this charismatic hero. It is said that Robin died in one of its rooms and that moments before his death he fired an arrow from the window and requested that he be buried wherever the arrow fell. That wish was granted, and his supposed grave lies within the grounds of Kirklees Hall.

As with so many legends, the distinction between truth and fiction is somewhat blurred but stories of his links with Kirklees extend far into history, while accounts of his exploits throughout Yorkshire have led many to conclude that he was in fact a Yorkshireman. It is quite feasible that he spent his youth in and around Wakefield.

An old verse tells us that:

The father of Robin a forester was,
And he shot with a lusty strong bow,
Two north country miles and an inch at a shoot
As the Pindar of Wakefield doth know.

Robin's childhood mischief brought him into confrontation with the Jolly Pindar of Wakefield. (A pindar's job was to impound and care for any stray animals by placing them in the pindar, or pound as it was sometimes called. He then had to trace the owners and recover the costs of detention and upkeep. The money was handed to the local court leet.) This pindar was a shepherd by occupation, and his duties as pindar were completed in his spare moments.

It seems that the young Robin Hood and two of his friends decided to rob the shepherd and steal the money he had collected in pindar fees, but the tough moorland shepherd thrashed them instead. It is said that this lesson was learned on one of the ancient sheep tracks of Craven, high in the dales of North Yorkshire.

There are no positive dates for Robin Hood's wanderings around England's largest county, but it is known that a relation of his was prioress at Kirklees. Some accounts say she was his cousin, while others claim she was an aunt. However, she was a prioress and may have been the first: if she *was* the first prioress of Kirklees, this dates her existence to the twelfth century.

Her name was Elizabeth de Stainton or Staynton, who had been born at Woolley, near Wakefield. Most accounts claim she was cousin to Robin Hood, but whether she was of similar age is not known. Upon her death she was buried in the cemetery to the south of the church along with two other nuns, and in 1706 her tombstone was discovered. The inscription ran: *'Douce J.H.U. de Nazaret Filz Dieu Tez Mercy a Elizabeth Stainton, Priores de cest maison'* – 'Sweet Jesus of Nazareth, Son of God, have mercy on Elizabeth Stainton, prioress of this house.'

Little is known of Elizabeth Stainton except that she was said to be 'a woman very skilful in physic and surgery' – or, in the words of her time, 'skilled in chirurgery'; in truth, a sort of medieval nurse. If she was indeed Robin's cousin or perhaps his aunt, we might assume that around 1155, or in the years that followed the date of the foundation of her priory, he was active in robbing the rich to give to the poor.

The snag with the myth is that there are several towns which claim to be either the birthplace or the early home of Robin Hood, with Nottingham, Sheffield, Doncaster and Wakefield each fielding some evidence. Even the

London Borough of Barnet has entered a rival claim, but it seems this is based on the theory that 'Barnsdale' (see later) should really read 'Barnet Vale'. In Staffordshire it was thought Robin Hood was really a villain called Alf, or Alfred de Hunterden, who roamed the forests around Penkridge some time after 1173.

The truth is that the name of Robin Hood crops up in many different parts of England in many different centuries and in many different situations. At least ten counties have place-names associated with him, including hills, wells, tumuli, inns, cliffs and sundry other places such as modern streets and roadside cafés. There is even a village which is named in his honour – it is the picturesque Robin Hood's Bay on the Yorkshire coast. With so many rival claims, it is not easy to determine which, if any, of the Robin Hoods is the man upon whom the legend is based.

Indeed, some believe that the name Robin Hood has distant links with Robin Goodfellow, a forest spirit or elf who had other names, such as Puck. He also appeared as a hob, a hobgoblin, a type of sun god, a Scandinavian deity, and even a barguest, Jack-o'-the-lantern and Will-o'-the-Wisp. In other words, Robin Hood may not have been human at all, but a forest sprite of some kind who has, over many generations become accepted as a real person. Perhaps he is a composite figure, an amalgamation of all the legends, heroic tales, elfs, goblins and sprites along with a liberal sprinkling of the myths of several centuries?

Add to these ingredients a dash of novels by famous authors, an epic poem, a hint of noble birth, some Hollywood films and a British TV series or two, and we have a super-hero of the kind that most spirited young men would wish to emulate.

The man called Robin Hood is an undoubted hero. Handsome, brave, talented and clever, he was chivalrous and thoroughly good. He tormented the evil people of the day, such as corrupt officials, bullies and evil-doers of every kind, and he was a church-going man too. A devout

Roman Catholic, he attended Mass every day and had a special devotion to the Virgin Mary. But he took money from the rich to give to the poor, which in legal terms made him a robber – 'but the gentlest there ever was'.

Some authorities firmly believe that the long-living legend began in the eleventh century, while others are equally firm that it all started in the twelfth, around the time of Richard I's reign (1189–99). But in one case-history of Robin Hood there is a definite starting-point with a legal foundation, and the town is York.

This early reference to Robin Hood does suggest he spent time in Yorkshire, even if he did carry out raids in Nottinghamshire and Derbyshire. Indeed, should the sheriff of Nottingham really be named the sheriff of Knottingley, which is a West Yorkshire town?

This version of the tale begins in 1225, when a Robin Hode failed to appear at York Assizes and was therefore declared an outlaw. The charge may have been one of rape, probably a false accusation made by a woman whom he had spurned, for he was a ladies' man, with many women competing for his attention. His age at the time of this allegation is not given, but this occurred seventy years after the foundation of Kirklees Priory and, as some accounts suggest that Robin was ninety when he died, this could be our man. That this Robin travelled the country could be established from the fact that in 1261 a Robin Hode appears in Berkshire, where he was described as a scoundrel. He is known to have made good use of the thick woodlands for cover as he moved around, and there is no doubt that, living rough as he did, he would need to steal food and cash in order to survive. But would he travel from York to Berkshire even if he was being hunted?

If this man is seen as the original Robin Hood, there is an equal or perhaps stronger claim which suggests that the entire legend begins some three-quarters of a century later. It implies that the city of Wakefield was the birthplace and home of the young Robin Hood. The difference in dates suggests that the Wakefield man was not the one who was outlawed in York. Nonetheless, the Wakefield man's life is of greater interest, because it suggests that the legendary Robin Hood was a real person and not a myth based on foreign sprites, sun gods or folk-stories.

The manor court rolls of Wakefield for the reign of Edward I (1272–1307) have revealed the existence of a forester called Adam Hood. He worked for Earl Warren, who was lord of the manor of Wakefield. In his role of forester, Adam Hood would also act as gamekeeper for the estate and would be skilled in the arts of tracking, hunting, killing and breeding all kinds of game and fish; he would know how to live in the woods and how to use a bow and arrow to best advantage. He and his wife produced a son around 1290, and they called him Robin, which was the shortened version of Robert. It is fairly certain that the boy Robin would be taught all these skills by his father, the assumption being that one day he would take over or at least work alongside his father. In his adolescence, young Robin was once fined 2 pence for stealing wood.

So was this man's son named in honour of the earlier Robin Hood, who perhaps, even by this time, had become a legend even if he did appear at York Assizes, or was this the actual youngster who was destined to become the famous outlaw? It is known, however, that the name Robin Hood was a very common one at that time, the equivalent almost of the modern John Smith or Joe Brown. Nonetheless, it is known that the Robert (Robin) Hood of Wakefield grew up and that in 1315, at the age of twenty-five, at Campsall between Wakefield and Doncaster, he married Matilda, who was 'a bonny fine maid of worthy degree'.

One account written in 1822 says she was Matilda Fitzwalter, daughter of the baron of Arlingford and that

Robin's real name was Robin Fitz-Ooth, Earl of Loxsley and Huntingdon; this is the name given in Nottingham's claim to be the birthplace of the outlaw (although Loxsley is a suburb of Sheffield) but this does not agree with the Wakefield name of the groom. There he was just Robin or Robert Hood. After their wedding, the couple leased a plot of land at Bickhill, near Wakefield. They paid 2 shillings for this, and it was ten yards long by five yards wide. There they constructed a five-bedroomed house; the site was near a medieval market and is near the present Bull Ring.

But it was not long before this Robin was recruited by the powerful earl of Lancaster to fight against Edward II (reign 1307–27). Robin had no alternative but to fight for the earl of Lancaster – the land which he had leased and upon which he had built his house had been signed over to the earl in compensation for Warren's seduction of the earl of Lancaster's wife, and the men of that estate were bound to fight for their landlord. Robin Hood was thirty-two when the battle was fought at Boroughbridge near Ripon in Yorkshire in 1322. Somewhat against general expectations, the king won.

Thomas, Earl of Lancaster, was taken prisoner and executed at Pontefract Castle, while his army all fled, now being regarded as rebels. The houses owned by the rebels were confiscated – and among them was a five-bedroomed house at Pickhill near Wakefield, the home of Robert and Matilda Hood. The couple were therefore homeless, and Robert was declared an outlaw. In his flight from the king, Robert assumed the name Robin, while Matilda called herself Marion, a name often given to those girls who were christened Matilda. And so, under their new identities, they fled into the forest to live as outlaws.

In the dales of Yorkshire there were acres and acres of forests, including the massive forest of Barnsdale. This covered an immense area of countryside and stretched south from Yorkshire to join the huge Sherwood Forest in Nottinghamshire. The name Sherwood comes from 'shire-wood', and the boundaries of three counties or shires were within its limits – Yorkshire, Nottinghamshire and Derbyshire. Each of these counties continues to claim links with the outlaw. Many survive in the names of locations which still bear his name, but just as Nottingham has its modern Maid Marion Way, so those names could have been added many years after his death. The forest of Barnsdale, which has now been reduced to a small wood just north of Doncaster, then contained one main village, Wentworth, just south of Pontefract. Today Wentworth is just off the A1 in Yorkshire between Pontefract and Doncaster.

Robin had two firm friends who accompanied him – one was a seven-foot-tall sailor called John Little, the other always dressed in red and so became known as 'Will Scarlet'. As Robin gathered more men about him in his constant endeavour to avoid capture by the king's men, so his daring exploits became the source of many stories, some true and some exaggerated.

Edward II took a personal and very active interest in the outlaw who was now becoming a hero. In 1323, the year after the Battle of Boroughbridge, he visited Plumpton Park near Harrogate, where the famous Plumpton or Plompton Rocks are now a tourist attraction. Plumpton Hall, however, lay between Ripon and Fountains Abbey, and it is uncertain at which of these locations the king stayed. Plumpton Hall is marked on modern maps.

The Plompton family was noted for its fighting men over six centuries ago, and it seems they had a lot in common with the king. While staying there, Edward commented upon the lamentable shortage of deer. One of the foresters said they had been poached and that the only way to catch the culprits was for the king and his men to ride into Sherwood Forest disguised as monks. This subterfuge would trap the villains. The young king did as suggested – and his party was quickly caught by Robin Hood and his merry men.

The king was robbed of his cash but immediately given half of it back before being invited to join the outlaws for a meal.

It seems the disguised king and his undercover men were well entertained, because he then revealed his identity and granted pardons for the outlaws, but only on condition that they enter his service. They did so and for a time abandoned the life of outlaws in the forests.

While searching old files in the Public Records Office in 1942, a researcher called J.M. Walker found an account of Edward II's domestic expenses. It included several references to Robin Hood's pay as a valet and some which referred to the pay of John Little, but this account also revealed that Robin Hood was unreliable – nine monthly entries indicated that he took a lot of time off, and on two occasions he was totally absent. It seems that he eventually found regular salaried employment rather boring, and so he returned to his former life in the greenwood forest. Thus began a second series of exploits which rapidly became the talking-point of the country people.

Because he was a mystery man, Robin soon became a legend. Some said he was truly a nobleman: the Sheffield people said he was born at Loxley, a suburb of that city, and that he was really the earl of Huntingdon, while Nottingham folk said he was Robin de Kyme, a son of a large landowning family who used a false name due to his criminal past, which included conviction for rape and robbery.

Whatever his origins, he did roam across Yorkshire, from Barnsdale to the coast, making good use of the covering layer of forest as he avoided those who might capture him.

Various parts of the Yorkshire Dales and Moors were visited by Robin Hood. He spent some time relaxing at the village now named Robin Hood's Bay, where he was useless as a fisherman. He had been loaned a boat by the widow of a fisherman but was highly unsuccessful at sea fishing, not even realizing that the lines had to be baited. It was while fishing, however, that he did make an impact upon the local people, when he saved the village from a raid by a marauding ship from France. His fighting skills captured the boat, which contained £12,000 – and he used the money to endow a seamen's hospital at Scarborough, a town he used to visit when relaxing around Fylingdales. The bay was not known as Robin Hood's Bay in his time, receiving this distinctive title only around 1532 in his honour.

Among other stories which link Robin Hood with Yorkshire is the tale of his combat with the man we have come to know as Little John and the other known as the 'curtal fryar', otherwise Friar Tuck.

In the first case, Robin was crossing a footbridge when he was confronted by a large man armed only with a staff. Robin threatened him with an arrow if he did not give way, but the huge man, some seven feet tall, responded that it would be cowardly to shoot a man armed only with a staff. Robin said that no man ever called him a coward, threw away his bow and arrows and cut himself a staff. The two men then fought on the narrow log which served as the bridge, and Robin was eventually knocked into the water. As he clambered out, he praised his adversary and blew his horn to summon his men; they had been in the woods and were horrified to discover their wet master. But Robin considered the big man to be brave and so invited him to join the Merry Men. The man was called John Little, and so his name was changed to Little John.

The following day, and further down the stream, Robin Hood was approaching Fountains Abbey when he espied a large, fat friar guarding the way. The friar was armed with a sword and wore a steel cap, but Robin approached him and demanded that the friar carry him over the stream. The friar agreed, but when they reached the bank, he said, 'Carry me back, or your life will not be for much!' Robin Hood agreed and struggled over with the huge man on his back, upon which Robin then demanded that the friar carry him over once more. But now, as the 'curtal fryar' reached the middle of the stream, he threw off Robin Hood, who got another soaking.

The two drew swords and fought 'from ten to four', as an old account says, while Robin's men watched from their hiding-places. Exhausted, Robin asked the friar to stay his sword and called his men by a blast of his horn; they emerged from the forest to help him – but the crafty friar whistled and a pack of savage hounds rushed to his side. It was an honourable draw, and the two adversaries shook hands and became friends – this was Friar Tuck, who then decided to leave Fountains Abbey to join the Merry Men.

The river in question was the River Skell, which rises in the Yorkshire Pennines and flows through the grounds of Fountains Abbey via Ripon and into the River Ure on its final part of the journey down Wensleydale. It flows past Plumpton Hall, only a mile or so from Fountains Abbey, which was another place visited by Robin Hood.

These and many other stories were told by word of mouth, and none was put into writing until 1377, when a reference to Robin Hood appears in William Langland's *Piers Plowman*. Alexandre Dumas did say that in 1304 Robin Hood was compared with William Wallace, the Scottish hero, but this date is doubtful and there were almost forty different ballads about Robin in the Middle Ages. The chief source of the stories is a long poem of almost 2,000 lines. Anonymously written around 1400, not many years after Robin Hood's death, it was not published until 1489. It has since formed the basis of countless books, films and articles about Robin Hood. It was called *A Lytell Geste of Robyn Hode*, and it created the character we know so well. I have found a further reference in 1549, in a sermon preached by Bishop Hugh Latimer before Edward VI. It seems that the fame of the outlaw was then so high that a parish church at which the bishop called was closed because the villagers were celebrating Robin Hood's Day. It transpires that 1 May was honoured as Robin Hood's Day, but the bishop does not identify the church.

In his sermon, Latimer said, 'I tarried there for half an hour or more, at last the key was found and one of the parish comes to me and says, "Sir, this is a busy day with us, we cannot hear you, it is Robin Hood's Day. The parish are gone abroad to gather for Robin Hood." It is no laughing matter my friends, it is a weeping matter, a heavy matter, under the pretence of gathering for Robin Hood, a traitor and a thief, to put out a preacher, to have his office less esteemed, to prefer Robin Hood before the ministration of God's word.'

The publication of *A Lytell Geste of Robyn Hode* may have caused this surge of interest among the people, and it might also have led to a number of name-changes in landmarks, Robin Hood's Bay being one example and perhaps the Robin Hood Tower on York's city walls – until 1622 this was called Frost Tower. The spreading legend may have given rise to the hundreds of Robin Hood sites throughout Yorkshire, Nottinghamshire and Derbyshire, as indeed it continues to do. There are many modern Robin Hood inns, cafés and streets which have no direct link with the outlaw.

But even the finest heroes must die, and so it was with Robin Hood. It might have been expected that the rough, tough and open-air life would take its toll upon the ageing outlaw and that he would have died through natural causes, but this was not so. His highly acclaimed defiance of authority had led to repeated clashes with the king, and it was the king's men who drove Robin Hood high into the hills of Yorkshire.

Hitherto, he and his Merry Men had been safe in the dales, and for a time he was allowed to remain there almost without any interference. But when he continued to take the king's deer, to anger the local bishops and lords of the manor, to upset the sheriffs of the region and to break all manner of laws, both local and national, he placed himself at risk. It mattered not that his efforts were for the good of the poor and needy.

In one final attempt to subdue the outlaw, King Edward (possibly Edward III by this time) sent one of his finest knights in pursuit of Robin Hood. His name was Sir William, and he was regarded as a trusty and worthy man. With a contingent of the best archers, he set off to hunt the outlaw and found evidence of his presence in the forests near Wakefield.

We are not told the precise circumstances of the battle, but we do know that, as a result, Robin Hood was hit and grievously wounded. But he was alive, and his men were able to carry him away from Sir William's men. He asked to be taken to his cousin's priory at Kirklees, for she was noted for her skills in tending the sick and injured.

The Merry Men agreed and took him there. He told them to save themselves – a large number of men in a nuns' priory was bound to raise suspicion, and so they departed and concealed themselves in the forests. But they did not abandon him. They waited in the greenwood, with Little John close at hand in case he was required to help his long-time friend.

Elizabeth Stainton received her cousin and allowed him to be placed in a small timbered room in what is now the gatehouse of Kirklees Hall. (It was then part of the priory and may have been her own lodgings.) It had three storeys, and Robin was placed in an upper room and locked in. Two differing accounts then attempt to find a motive for what Elizabeth did. One said that, in his most daring outlaw raids, Robin had killed a friend of hers, or possibly a relation or even an illicit suitor, and that she was now able to take her revenge. Another account suggests that she was a religious maniac who regarded

her wayward cousin as an enemy of all holy people and
that she saw it as her duty to bring his evil life to an end.
Perhaps she misunderstood his dealings with corrupt
priests? Or was it all a tragic accident?

The treatment of those times for many illnesses and
diseases was to attach blood-sucking leeches to the patient
and allow them to draw out the bad blood. Elizabeth
attached a large number of leeches to the already
weakened Robin Hood, locked him in the tiny room and
left him to bleed. Unfortunately he bled to death. It was a
slow and lingering departure from the world, but it was
some time before Robin realized his impending fate. He
had with him his trusty horn, the one he had used so
many times to summon the help of his Merry Men, and so,
the moment he realized the truth of his predicament, he
tried to blow it.

The old verse says, 'He blew out weak blasts three', but
it was enough to reach the ears of Little John, waiting
patiently among the trees. He recognized the weakness by
saying, 'I fear my master is near dead, he blows so
wearily.'

But Little John tried to save him. He had to break into
the priory, smashing several locks on the way, and he now
realized what the evil woman had done. He prayed that he
would be in time to save his master and that he might be
allowed to burn down the nunnery. When he arrived at
the room in which Robin lay dying on the floor, he
explained his intentions. But Robin would have no
violence against a woman.

'I have never hurt a fair maid in all my time,' he said,
'and I am not going to begin now. Give me my bow and
one arrow. I am dying, John, and wherever the arrow falls,
there shall my grave be.'

And so it was. Some accounts say that Robin fired two
arrows – the first fell into the River Calder and was carried
uselessly downstream, and so he asked for a second. That
one, fired with all the skill of England's most famous

bowman, albeit with signs of weakness, fell among some trees on a lofty piece of rocky ground. Robin then expired. As requested, he was buried there. Although there is no public access, the grave is there today, an enclosure of stone surrounded by iron railings, and there was once a cross in the centre with a block of stone at the back bearing this legend:

Hear undernead dis laitl stean
Laiz robert earl of Huntingtun
near arcer ver az he so geud
An pipl kauld him robin heud
Sike utlauz as he and hiz men
Vil england nivr si agen.

Over the years, the stone surrounds were broken and the inscription quoted above disappeared with the passage of time and the effect of the weather. A copy of the old version was found among some papers belonging to a Dr Gale who was once the dean of York, and its modern translation is:

Here underneath this little stone,
Lies Robert, Earl of Huntingdon,
No archer was as he so good
And people called him Robin Hood.
Such outlaws as he and his men
Will England never see again.

Upon Robin's death, his Merry Men split up and fled. It is said that the entire group comprised over one hundred men but, fearing they would be captured and executed or imprisoned without the leadership of Robin Hood, some went overseas to Flanders, France and Spain and some even headed for Rome. But some remained in the forests. Will Scarlet went to live at Blidworth in Nottinghamshire and is reputedly buried there, while Little John remained in Yorkshire and died in peace: he is buried at Hathersage, over the border in Derbyshire. His grave is at the church of St Michael and All Angels at Hathersage and is maintained by the Ancient Order of Foresters.

The whereabouts or circumstances of Maid Marion at this terrible time are not recorded, and some authorities suggest she was never a part of Robin Hood's adventures, being a figment of some author's imagination and incorporated into the legend around 1500; some believe she was not part of the forest group until 1800! It is claimed, however, that she lived at Blidworth.

There are doubts about the grave too. One researcher said that the earth beneath it is solid rock and that it could never have been dug to form a grave, while another claims that, when the grave was examined during the last century, it was empty. These are contradictory statements. The latter does suggest it was a grave, but whose? If it was Robin's, thieves might have raided it to carry off the famous skeleton. Yet another account says a skeleton was discovered there some time ago but that it was by then little more than dust and not identifiable.

Yet another writer has stated that the grave is a fake and that the supposed epitaph was also a fake; as that inscription has long since vanished from the stonework, no one can examine the work to determine its age. But that epitaph also contained a date. It said Robin Hood died on 24 December 1247. If this was true, this was not the same man who was born near Wakefield in 1290 and who married Matilda in 1315. But it could have been the Robin Hood who was outlawed at York Assizes in 1225!

So, having examined the theories, can we say that Robin Hood was murdered? Elizabeth Stainton pleaded her innocence and said she had never intended to kill him, adding that his weakness had been greater than she had realized and that his death was an unfortunate accident. No one can prove or disprove either of the theories.

At the time of writing, there are difficulties over access

to the site of the grave, for it has been suggested that a clergyman of the Church of England should bless the tomb as a sign of forgiveness. Maybe Robin would object to this, for he would be a Roman Catholic; in his time, the Church of England did not exist – it was founded more than three centuries after the suggested date of his death.

In any case, the present owner of the land which contains the supposed grave, Lady Margarete Armytage, will not allow any access to the site. Thus the legendary grave of Robin Hood remains secure from modern attention and examination, and so it cannot, at the moment, provide any further information.

So was Robin Hood of Sherwood Forest a real person? If he was, there is a wealth of evidence to suggest he was a Yorkshireman, but the truth remains as elusive as was the outlaw himself.

4   The Deaths of Two Lady Saints

An act of murder is depicted in the stained-glass windows of two Anglican parish churches in the Yorkshire dales. One is at Middleham in Wensleydale and the other is at Giggleswick in Ribblesdale. In another instance, the dreadful penalty inflicted on a Catholic York woman is commemorated in her shrine in York's ancient and beautiful street called The Shambles.

In each case, the victim was a young woman. One was St Alkelda of Middleham and the other St Margaret Clitherow of York.

There is a mystery surrounding Alkelda, whom some believe to have been a Saxon princess. Her killers were two Danish women who either strangled her with a scarf or neckerchief or alternatively used her long hair to choke the life out of her. As the murder may have been committed more than a thousand years ago, it is not known whether the killers were ever brought to justice, because reliable records of the actual event do not exist. But the name of the victim lives on, which makes us believe that Alkelda must have been an important or a well-loved person. In fact, in the minds of some, she is now a saint.

Although the name Alkelda does not appear in lists of canonized saints, those two Yorkshire Dales churches honour her as such, and this raises the questions – who was Alkelda and why was she murdered so cruelly?

The curious stained-glass reminders of Alkelda's sad and untimely departure from earthly life are not her only testimonial, for other reminders of her are to be found in Middleham. The church itself is dedicated only partly to her – it is known as the Church of St Mary and St Alkelda. Her bones are said to have been buried beneath the nave. Nearby there is also a well which is named after her – St Alkelda's Well, and this was once accredited with the ability to work miracles and cure ailments, especially weak eyes.

The Church of St Alkelda at Giggleswick, high in Ribblesdale, is yet another reminder of Alkelda and her untimely end, but this village does not claim to be the scene of the saint's life and death: it merely honours her.

By the flight of the proverbial crow, these churches are some twenty-five miles apart, although by road it would be a far lengthier and very picturesque journey because they are separated by the bulk of some of the highest peaks of the Pennine range. Between them stand the heights of Buckden Pike (2,302 feet) and Great Whernside (3,210 feet), as well as hundreds of square miles of deserted and inhospitable moorland and fells. To reach the other side of these fells requires a long trek through high dales, steep passes and remote stone-built villages.

Even if St Alkelda's two parish churches are separated with such determination, it is interesting that no other church in England, nor probably in the world, is dedicated to her. In order to examine her life, we must visit Middleham.

The village found itself featured in the national headlines in 1985, when a medieval jewel was found buried in a field near the castle. Exquisitely crafted in gold, it had a sapphire in the front above a scene of the crucifixion, while the back featured the nativity. The jewel, which was not declared treasure trove, was later sold by auction at Sotheby's in London and realized over £1.4 million. This exquisite and unique example of medieval art is now known as 'the

Middleham Jewel'.

But Middleham is no stranger to events of national interest. For such a small place, it boasts an astonishing history which dates to Roman times, a castle built by the Normans, a powerful link with King Richard III, who lived here for eleven years, and modern strings of racehorses which regularly win at all the major courses in Britain. In spite of this, it remains a quiet and peaceful dales village, although some claim it is Yorkshire's smallest town.

The village is a pleasant blend of ancient stone-built houses and inns set among steep streets, and it boasts two market squares in addition to its castle and fascinating church. One square contains an old market cross which has been restored, while the other is near the castle and contains an old bull-ring close to the curious Swine Cross. With two flights of steps, this bears a carved animal which is difficult to identify due to the damage: it might have been the boar of Richard III or the bear of the Warwicks.

Or it might be simply a pig, informing traders that this was where pigs were bought and sold. The larger old markets had such crosses – there were fish crosses, butter crosses, bread crosses, sheep crosses and so on, each easily identifiable to inform the illiterate traders where to buy and sell their goods. The original ones were shaped like crosses to add a holy blessing to the proceedings, but later ones were in any shape and form, some even sporting roofs and upstairs compartments while retaining the name of cross.

At almost every corner, one is made aware of the links between Richard III and Middleham. Village shops sell books and souvenirs, for here they claim the king was not as evil as portrayed in history. It was to Middleham that the future King Richard III came when he was only eleven. He stayed at the castle, where he was trained in military tactics, arms and chivalry; his host was his cousin, the Earl of Warwick, who was known as 'the Kingmaker'. During his time at the castle, Richard met and fell in love with

Warwick's daughter, Anne, but they were later separated. In 1472 she did become his bride, and in 1483 she became his queen.

Only two years later Richard was killed at the Battle of Bosworth still suspected of complicity in the murder of two princes, Edward V and his brother Richard, Duke of York, in the Tower of London. It was when Richard declared them illegitimate that he was able to secure the throne, but these notes are not to explain the truth or otherwise of Richard III's possible involvement in a double murder.

After his marriage to Anne, Richard lived in Middleham Castle for a further eleven years, and their only child, Edward, was born in what became known as the Prince's Tower, while his nursery was next door, over the bakehouse. He was Prince of Wales and died at Middleham Castle at the age of eight.

At the time, this castle was one of the finest in the north, the stronghold of the Nevilles, and its famous keep is one of the largest, with walls ten feet thick and fifty-five feet high. Today it is in the care of English Heritage and is a focal-point for visitors, just as in the time of the Nevilles it was the administrative centre for the north of England.

The fine church, parts of which date to Norman times, also contains reminders of Richard III and illustrates the tremendous historical background of Middleham. Much of the building dates to the fourteenth century, and one of the tombs is that of Robert, the abbot of nearby Jervaulx Abbey, whose remains were brought here during Henry VIII's destruction of the monasteries.

All around Middleham are panoramic views of Wensleydale, with the River Ure glistening in the dale below and a backcloth of the rising fells and tiny, isolated villages and farms. The bustle created by the medieval barons and their friends has long gone, and it is now the sort of place to which a saint would wish to come to live a life of peace and prayer.

At the time of Alkelda, however, it was probably not so quiet. The Danes may have been invading the area, raping, pillaging and killing as they rampaged through the countryside and among their targets were any Christian people. In their terms, anything linked in any way to Christianity had to be destroyed. In the years just before 867 the Danes overran Yorkshire. They destroyed many religious establishments in the county, including famous ones such as St Cuthbert's monastery at Crayke, St Cedd's at Lastingham and St Hilda's at Whitby. This old account sums up the atmosphere of the time: 'They [the Danes] could conceive no greater pleasure than to feast their eyes upon the flames of villages which they had plundered and their ears with the groans of their captives expiring under torture. Their route was marked with the mangled corpses of monks, nuns and priests whom they had massacred ...'

But even if the Danes were not running amok, there might have been other rogues at large, for one's existence in those early times was dangerous and precarious. Human life was regarded as a cheap commodity at the hands of those who killed for greed or pleasure.

Most accounts of the life of St Alkelda, however, subscribe to the belief that she fell victim to two Danish women who strangled her and that her death occurred no later than the tenth century. The motive for this crime is unknown.

So who was Alkelda?

From the very meagre information available, she may have been either an Anglo-Saxon princess or a noble-woman, or she might have been a very ordinary but very decent local girl. We know nothing of her parents, her family or her work, but it does seem that she lived in Middleham, which was then probably called Medelei, and that she was a very good-living girl. One thing that emerges is that the people of a parish as small as this would accredit meritworthy local people who died a 'good' death with the title of 'saint'. They did not await any official confirmation, declaration or canonization by the Pope, and this was especially the case when a person died a martyr's death. At that time, therefore, many local people were known as saints even though their causes for canonization were never formalized by the Vatican's processes.

If the stories are true and if the stained-glass windows at Middleham and Giggleswick give a true account, Alkelda did die a martyr's death, and she was known as a saint, if only in Middleham or perhaps in a wider area which included Wensleydale and other parts of the Yorkshire Dales.

This can be borne out by the fact that her name does not appear in most of the reference books of saints, although there is a very brief note in the *Oxford Dictionary of Saints*. In this case, she is linked to St Arild, the implication being that this is one saint with two names. The fact is there is no link between Arild and Alkelda, and I understand this error has been acknowledged.

Arild has no connection with the north of England. She died at Kingston-by-Thornbury in Gloucestershire when she was decapitated by a tyrant called Muncius. After the Norman Conquest, her bones were transferred to Gloucester Abbey, where her shrine became noted for its miracles. She was depicted in the east window of the abbey, and a statue was erected in the Lady Chapel. Two churches are named in her honour, neither of which lies in Yorkshire.

The lack of information about Alkelda does lead to a query as to whether or not she did exist. In his scholarly series of books *The Buildings of England*, Sir Nikalaus Pevsner writes of Alkelda in the volume dealing with the North Riding of Yorkshire, 'It is entirely unknown who she was.'

But the church authorities of ancient Middleham would disagree, because, they claimed, after her death she was buried in the nave of the church, and more modern churchmen claim that a piece of stone in the wall of the vestry is part of her tombstone. Indeed, an inscription on a pillar within the church continues to confirm that she is buried beneath the nave.

Some years ago her grave was the site of a curious ceremony. It became the custom, even until the final years of the last century, for certain farm rents to be paid over St Alkelda's tomb. The money was placed on a stone table in the middle of the nave, and apparently some ancient annual doles were also paid from the same table. It seems that the table was removed some time before 1888, and the customs involving doles and rents ended.

So far as the Giggleswick parish church is concerned, it suggests that Alkelda was a Saxon lady who lived in Yorkshire, and it reiterates the belief that she was murdered by two Danish women. As at Middleham, that murder is commemorated in a stained-glass window. This church, however, in its own research found no mention of Alkelda in the chronicles of the Finchale monks, even though Finchale Priory held the advowson of the living of Giggleswick for 3½ centuries. The first mention of Alkelda, so far as Giggleswick is concerned, arises in the will of James Carr in 1528. He expressed a wish to be buried 'in the church of Gigleswicke of the Holie and Blessed Virgin Saint Alkelda'.

But perhaps the most important clue as to her existence or otherwise lies in St Alkelda's Well at Middleham. Those who suggest that Alkelda never existed as a real person claim that she is a mere myth, and a strong case for this belief can be based on the well that bears her name.

In Yorkshire, the local name for a well is often 'keld' – in the moors and dales, there are many names such as Keldholme, Keld Head or just Keld. The Anglo-Saxon word for 'holy' was '*halig*', and their word for a well was *kelda*. Thus a holy well was '*halig kelda*'. The well at Middleham was for years known as *halig kelda*, when such wells were the meeting-places of the wapentake. In the area around Middleham, the word lives on in the locality known as Hallikeld, and one of the wapentakes in the Honour of nearby Richmond was called Halikeldshire in 1157, later known as Hallikeld. The name was eventually given to the Hallikeld Petty Sessional Division of the Richmond district, and the name continues to crop up in house or farm names, such as Halikeld House. Sometimes a double 'l' is used, and sometimes a single one.

In appreciating the changes of language and pronunciation, it does not require much imagination to see the striking similarity between *halig kelda*, Alkelda and Hallikeld.

But from this can we presume that Alkelda was not a real person, merely a holy or 'magic' well? Those ancient wells, with their pure water supply, were often considered magic wells or wishing wells because their waters did not cause illness. In truth, they were usually the sole supply of unpolluted water, and their 'powers' were nothing more than a lack of pollution. Some primitive people thought they contained holy spirits, and over the years it would be easy to accredit a well with the holy powers of a saintly, miracle-working person. As the stories of the well's miracles passed from person to person by word of mouth over almost a thousand years, it is easy to see how the myth grew. And, in time, when the story was put into writing, the existence of a mythical person could so easily be regarded as fact. So was this magic well the origin of the name Alkelda?

If Alkelda did not exist, therefore, the murder never happened and she was never martyred.

But is it feasible that two hard-headed Yorkshire communities would name their churches after a local holy well and give that well the status of a saint?

The answer might lie in Yorkshire today, because, when I was researching this mystery, I received a letter from a 10-year-old girl in a village near my home. She is called Alkelda. And it is known that some people do name their children after favourite places, flowers, trees or stones. There are many girls with such names as Beverley, Hazel, Rose, Ruby and so forth, so if modern people can follow that trend, why should not an Anglo-Saxon family have done likewise?

This made me realize that some proud Anglo-Saxon parents might have given birth to a little girl and then named her after the most famous place in their village, the holy well – the *halig kelda*. And just suppose that she grew up to be a holy and good young woman, a devout Christian but a pretty and wise girl too, who suddenly found herself confronted by two hateful Danish women determined to exterminate all Christian women? That young girl called Alkelda might have been murdered more than a thousand years ago, and the local people might have elevated her to the status of saint.

If so, the parish churches of Giggleswick and Middleham might be the only reminders of her true sacrifice.

The life of the second saint, Margaret Clitherow, is well documented, for there is no doubt about her existence and suffering. Although she is York's most recent saint, her place of burial remains a mystery.

She was born Margaret Middleton at York in 1556 where her father was a chandler, dealing in wax candles. Margaret, a Protestant, grew up during the aftermath of the Reformation, when anyone practising the Roman Catholic faith was liable to confiscation of their property, imprisonment or even execution. Her father was eminent in the city of York, once being elected sheriff, but he died in 1567. Margaret attended church at St Martin-le-Grand in Coney Street but had little interest in the religious difficulties of the time.

When Margaret was fifteen she married John Clitherow, who was a widower with two young children; he was a butcher, and his home was in The Shambles at York. The word 'Shambles' indicates a place used by butchers, and this was a smelly street littered with offal and blood, but Margaret settled into married life and by all contemporary accounts was happy. Popular in the area, she was bright, sociable and very efficient in her household duties.

But the religious struggle was fermenting; it must have been both confusing and frightening to the ordinary people as the state tried to crush the old Catholic faith, and the Protestant Queen Elizabeth I demanded that her subjects acknowledge her as Supreme Head of the Church.

Many violently disagreed with this, and an uprising of northern barons tried to put her off the throne. They were arrested and executed for treason, one of them being the earl of Northumberland. This bigoted cruelty had a profound effect upon Margaret Clitherow.

Meanwhile, John Clitherow became a special constable in York and joined in the hunt against Catholics while his young wife began to study the Catholic faith. At the age of eighteen she was converted to that faith. Two years later she was named officially as a 'recusant' – a person who refused to attend Protestant services. Some Catholics did attend these services in order to maintain their property and avoid trouble, but a hard core steadfastly refused. Margaret Clitherow was now one of those few.

She visited captive priests in York Castle, and later, when it became treason for a priest to teach Catholicism in England, she harboured them in her house in The Shambles. There they remained until a secret journey could be arranged for them to reach their English missions. For her work in assisting Catholics, Margaret was fined several times – and her husband willingly paid most of the fines. He did not try to stop her activities, and some believe he may have been a secret Catholic who outwardly conformed to the new religion. Indeed, he had once been a Catholic, and his brother was a Catholic priest. In public, however, he said Catholics were of evil disposition and did his utmost to show his support for the new and official English faith.

Next door to the Clitherows there lived a secret Catholic who agreed that a Mass centre should be established between the two houses. It would be hidden in the top floor between the two properties, and the entrance would be in the neighbour's house. There would also be access from Margaret's house via a narrow channel that only a child could use. The penalty for attending Mass was six months' imprisonment, so it was hoped this new Mass centre would escape the notice of the authorities.

About this time persecution of Catholics was increased, and between July 1582 and May 1583 five priests were arrested in York and dragged over Ouse Bridge and up Micklegate for execution on the Knavesmire, now the home of York Racecourse. A memorial stone marks the site of the martyrs' deaths.

During this period, Margaret was imprisoned, remaining in York Castle from March 1583 until May 1584. The law had been strengthened and now said that anyone harbouring a Catholic priest was liable to the death penalty. When Margaret was released from prison, therefore, she was kept under close observation by the authorities. But she was so well loved by all the people of York, Catholic and Protestant alike, that no one would inform against her, nor would they act as witnesses for any prosecution. In an attempt to frighten her into ceasing her activities, her husband was summoned to the Manor House for interview but he told Margaret what had transpired, saying he must return to the Manor House for further interrogation after dinner. While he was there, a priest had arrived at the Clitherow house, and Margaret advised him to leave, for his own safety, as she feared reprisals by the authorities. She was right, because that same day her house was raided and searched.

The secret Mass centre was not discovered, but the sheriff and councillors noticed a small boy in the house.

He was twelve years old and Flemish, a guest of the Clitherows, and the councillors stripped him and threatened to beat him unless he showed them the entrance to the Mass centre. This he did and they found the remains of a recent meal, evidence of a fleeing priest. Margaret was arrested and the boy told them more about the Masses, the Catholic priests and all who used the centre.

On Monday 14 March 1586 Margaret Clitherow was called to her trial, knowing that the verdict was a foregone conclusion and that she would be executed on the Knavesmire. The charge was that, 'She had harboured and kept Jesuit and seminary priests, traitorous to the Queen's Majestie and her laws, and that she had heard Mass and such like.'

There were two judges, Judge Rhodes, who had participated in the trial of Mary, Queen of Scots, and Judge Clinch; it was he who asked how she pleaded. She replied that she knew of no crime of which she was guilty. The judge then accused her of harbouring and keeping Jesuits and priests, enemies to Her Majesty. Margaret said she had harboured only the Queen's friends.

The judge then asked the formal question, 'How will you be tried?' The anticipated answer was 'By God and the jury', but Margaret insisted that, as she had committed no crime, she required no trial. Further attempts were made to persuade her to plead, and Judge Clinch reminded her that the only evidence against her was that of a small boy. She retorted that a child could be made to say anything with an apple or a rod. The judge continued to plead with her to agree to a trial, the angry Rhodes accusing her of harlotries with the priests. But she refused, and it is felt she did so to protect anyone else who might be involved with her work. In so doing, she knew she must suffer the infamous torture which was designed to force people to make a plea. It was known as *'peine forte et dure'* and involved laying the victim on the floor with a sharp stone under the spine, and then placing a number of increasingly heavy weights upon them until either they made a plea or they were crushed to death.

Margaret was led away to prison to await this awful treatment as others tried to make her accept the trial, but she refused. At 8 a.m. on Friday 25 March 1586 (which was then New Year's Day under the calendar of the time), she was taken to the Toll Booth at York which then stood beside the river near the Micklegate end of the present Ouse Bridge. She was bare-footed, bare-headed and bare-legged. A huge crowd had gathered and all wanted to speak with her, but she quietly knelt and prayed. Her executioners then took her and bound her hands to two posts, spread-eagled her on the floor and placed the required pointed stone beneath her spine. Then they began to place the weights upon her stomach and body.

It took her fifteen minutes to die in agony. She was thirty years old. Her body was buried in a dunghill somewhere in the city, but it was found six weeks later by some Catholics. It had not putrefied, and they removed it and carried it 'one long day's journey' away, to bury it with due honour.

Almost four centuries later, on 25 October 1970, after a meticulous examination of her life and motives, Margaret Clitherow was declared by Pope John Paul II to be a saint. The shrine of St Margaret Clitherow remains in The Shambles, York, although it may not be in her original home, and her place of burial remains a mystery.

5   Knaresborough –
The Trial of Eugene Aram

Even today, questions are asked about the guilt of Eugene Aram as scholars attempt to decide whether or not he should have been convicted of murder. There remains a deep interest in this case, even though Aram was executed over 230 years ago. The case has become a classic in the realms of Yorkshire crime because one of the key elements concerns a lack of proof of the identity of the body upon which the case depended. It was that omission that the accused man drew to the attention of those who tried him, and one additional but little-known aspect of the case is that it has left another unsolved mystery.

The alleged victim was Daniel Clark, a cobbler in Knaresborough. He was born in that Yorkshire town of good parents, but little is known of him except that he was married in January 1744 or 1745. His wife was a member of the Foster family of Embsay near Skipton, and she had a fortune of £300, a substantial sum at that time. The newly wed Mr and Mrs Clark were highly thought of in Knaresborough, and an old account says that Daniel Clark 'lived in good credit'.

Eugene Aram was a schoolmaster in the town, a clever man by all accounts, but it appears that Aram and Clark, together with another man called Richard Houseman, entered upon some kind of plan to obtain goods by fraud and then sell them.

When Clark disappeared shortly afterwards, it was

assumed by the townspeople that he had absconded with the stolen goods. Some thought he had absconded with his wife's money, but there were darker allegations about the fate of Clark, perhaps prompted by suspicions voiced by no less a person than Aram's wife. Despite the gossip, however, plus some proof of the trio's frauds, the mystery of Clark's disappearance remained unsolved until thirteen or fourteen years later. When a body was found at Knaresborough, it was rumoured to be that of Daniel Clark. As a result, Aram and Houseman were charged with having murdered him, but Houseman was acquitted and promptly gave damning evidence against Eugene Aram. Aram was convicted and executed.

It is Aram's name that lives on, those of the victim and Houseman being almost forgotten, and the name of Eugene Aram is now part of the folklore of Knaresborough. It ranks alongside that of Mother Shipton, the town's famous prophetess, and Blind Jack, Knaresborough's legendary road-maker. So why does the case of Eugene Aram continue to create such interest?

Eugene Aram was born at Ramsgill, a small village in Nidderdale, in 1704. He referred to the valley as 'Netherdale' but the house no longer stands. His father was from Nottinghamshire and was a gardener of great ability, an expert in botany and draughtsmanship. For a time he worked for the bishop of London, Dr Compton, and he was recommended to the owner of Newby Hall near Ripon, Sir Edward Blackett. Aram senior served in this capacity for more than thirty years, and the gardens of the extended Newby Hall continue to be renowned for their colour, range and splendour. When Sir Edward died, Mr Aram went to work for Sir John Ingilby of Ripley and later died in that service. Ripley Castle remains in the hands of the Ingilbys.

The Aram family were from a good background. There were several lords of a village once called Haram or Aram on the Yorkshire banks of the River Tees, and the name

Aram appeared among those who had been charitable to St Mary's Abbey in York. Although Aram's family was originally from Yorkshire, his ancestors moved to Nottinghamshire and settled at Aram Park near Newark-on-Trent. In the time of Edward III they owned land in the area, this property later being transferred – for reasons not known – to the ownership of Lord Lexington. One Aram was professor of divinity at Oxford and died at York, while others became high sheriffs of the county. Another ancestor, Thomas Aram of Gray's Inn, was one of Queen Anne's commissioners and married the heiress of Sir John Coningsby of Hertfordshire. It seems there was good breeding in Eugene Aram.

When he was five or six years old, he moved with his mother from Ramsgill to live at Skelton, the village adjoining the lands of Newby Hall. Then his father bought a cottage in Bondgate, Ripon, and the family moved there; it seems that Eugene later inherited that cottage and raised money by a mortgage upon it.

It was at Ripon that Eugene Aram attended school, and he proved a bright and clever pupil. At the age of thirteen or fourteen he joined his father as a gardener at Newby Hall until the death of Sir Edward Blackett. Being a solitary youth, he found solace in reading, and it was here that his love of literature was nurtured. He spent all his time reading and studying and discovered his aptitude for mathematics. In his father's library, he found many books on the subject, and he must have impressed his employer's family because Mr Christopher Blackett asked him to go to London to serve as a book-keeper in a financial institution. Eugene did go to London but two years later caught smallpox. Very ill, he returned home and was bedridden for eighteen months; afterwards he was regarded as a weakling and walked with a stoop. After his recovery, however, having mastered mathematics, he turned to poetry, literature and history. In his own words, he said, 'Their charms quite destroyed all the heavier penalties of numbers and lines.'

It seems his learning led to an appointment as a teacher in a school in Nidderdale, probably at Middlesmoor. Here he was married in 1731, and his daughter was baptized in Middlesmoor church; she was later buried there. But the marriage was unhappy. In fact, when he was in prison, he said the misconduct of his wife had led to his prosecution, followed by 'this infamy and this sentence'. Others said he treated his innocent, industrious wife in an infamous, inhuman manner.

Between his appointment at this village school and his conviction for murder, it seems Aram became obsessed with learning. It has even been suggested that, had he not entered the history books as a murderer, he might have done so as a classical scholar and writer. He mastered English grammar, then Greek and Latin, learning the classics by heart. He read Hesiod, Homer, Theocritus, Herodotus and Thucydides.

During these pursuits he received an offer of another teaching post. This was at Knaresborough, the offer coming from a good friend called William Norton. Aram began teaching there in 1734 and was well esteemed and liked. But he remained dissatisfied with his standard of learning and now began to study Hebrew, collecting between eight and ten different Hebrew grammars. He bought a Bible and studied the entire Pentateuch and later became what he described as 'a tolerable master of French'. He went to London to work for a time, now specializing in Latin, teaching the subject for the Revd Painblanc in Piccadilly, and later found alternative employment for a time at Hayes in Sussex as writing master to a gentlewoman.

It seems he worked for some time in the south of England, transcribing every Act of Parliament registered in Chancery, and then he went to Lynn, in Norfolk, having made further studies of botany, heraldry and antiquities, as well as the Arabic, Chaldee and Celtic tongues. (Chaldee was the Aramaic language used in the Old Testament.) He studied the dialects of the Celtic tongues and found a surprising affinity between them and Greek, Hebrew and Latin, so much so that he decided to compile a lexicon of more than 3,000 words he had collected.

During his time at Lynn, he was loved by his pupils and their families. While there, he was described as a man of calm countenance, with delicate health and a stoop; he muttered to himself, which was regarded as a sign of his massive intellect, but he was always poor because he spent all his money on books. He was a man of the mildest character, and it was said by Lord Lytton that he would turn aside from a worm in his path. He had high morals, gentleness and patience. His accomplishments were far greater than those of anyone of his background.

It was while Aram was teaching at Lynn in Norfolk that his entire life, along with his academic studies, was ruined. He was arrested on suspicion of having committed a murder which had occurred almost fourteen years earlier at Knaresborough in the Yorkshire Dales.

The constable who executed the warrant at Lynn was called John Barker, and he went to the school to arrest Aram, first having to establish that this teacher was in fact the man named in the warrant. Initially Aram denied all links with Knaresborough, and he denied knowing a man called Daniel Clark but the constable had a witness waiting outside the door, and that witness knew Aram by sight. And so he was arrested and conveyed to Knaresborough to stand trial.

The incident which had led to this arrest was the discovery of a body at Thistle Hill, Knaresborough. On 1 August 1758 some workmen digging for stone to supply a limekiln uncovered the corpse. They were digging near the edge of the cliff when, about a yard or so down they discovered the bone of a human arm. Further digging produced a leg and then an entire body, which, according to evidence at the time, appeared to have been buried double.

This discovery reminded the townspeople of the mysterious disappearance of Daniel Clark some thirteen or fourteen years earlier, and it was recalled that no other Knaresborough person had mysteriously vanished since that time. Because Eugene Aram had also left the town some thirteen or fourteen years before this discovery, suspicion fell upon him, for it was known he had been involved in some rather odd business dealings with Clark. But another acquaintance of both these men remained in the town – this was a Jew called Richard Houseman who was a flax-dresser. Aram's wife, Anna, also lived in Knaresborough, and it was recalled that after Clark's disappearance she had made allegations to her friends that she knew enough to hang her husband …

The discovery of the bones led to an inquest being held, and witnesses were called. One of them, a Mr Yeates, said he had been walking over Thistle Hill shortly after the time of Clark's disappearance and recalled having seen a freshly dug place of the size that might contain the body of a 12-year-old child. He had been shown the place where the bones were found and identified it as the same place. A second witness, Barbara Leatham of Knaresborough, gave similar evidence.

Then Mrs Aram was called to give her account of the events of thirteen or fourteen years earlier, and her testimony was most condemnatory. It supported the rumours and allegations of fraud by Aram, Clark and Houseman.

This is the story that emerged.

It seemed that soon after Clark's marriage in January 1744 or 1745, Eugene Aram and Richard Houseman decided to raise money by fraud, probably to settle some loans they had arranged among themselves. What is unclear is which of them was the originator of this hapless scheme, for, being well-known local men, their offences were sure to be discovered.

Nonetheless, they went ahead. They needed the services of a front man, someone who was known and trusted in the town. Clark, newly married and highly regarded by the local people, was ideal. Somehow Aram and Houseman persuaded him to go along with their plot. The scheme was to collect valuables from the householders and businesses and sell them for cash. Clark, using his recent marriage as a reason for wanting the goods on loan, did the canvassing.

On 7 February 1744 or 1745, therefore, Clark went from house to house in Knaresborough, persuading people to lend him table linen, bedding, drapery, woollen goods, clothes and furniture until he was able to obtain his own. Then he went to some local inns and obtained pewter pots, silver tankards, plates and other objects, saying he was having friends in to supper and did not have sufficient tableware of his own. He also obtained some ale and liquors on the strength of this story. One account says he obtained three tankards, four silver pint pots, a silver milk pot, a ring set with an emerald and two brilliant diamonds, another with three rose diamonds, a third with a heart-shaped amethyst and six plain rings, eight watches, two snuff boxes, two volumes of *Chambers' Dictionary* and six bound volumes of Pope's *Homer*.

Then, having obtained all these goods through a plausible lie, Clark vanished. It was assumed he had run off with all these goods or with his wife's money. But Aram's wife had not been quiet. She had gossiped to the effect that she could hang her husband if she was so minded ...

People grew suspicious and, after some powerful rumours had circulated the town, it was decided to search for the missing goods. Some were found at Houseman's, and some buried velvets were located in Aram's garden, but as none of the silver ware or valuables was discovered, it strengthened the belief that Clark had hidden the things he did not want to carry with him, using his friends' premises for this purpose, and that he had run off with the valuable items. Appeals for information, including advertisements in the local papers, produced no sightings of Clark and no recovery of the missing items.

But even then Aram fell under suspicion of having been an accomplice in Clark's fraud. It was known that he owed money, and a summons was issued to have him arrested for debt. This was done as a means of holding him while further process was prepared for a charge of his being an accomplice in defrauding some people of Knaresborough. Aram was known to be a poor but clever man, and everyone expected him to be gaoled, but when he was arrested for debt, he paid off the sum of £50, much to the surprise of everyone, and later paid off his mortgage on the family house in Bondgate, Ripon. Then, after his release from custody, Eugene Aram vanished from Knaresborough. What the local people did not realize was that he obtained several teaching positions throughout the south of England.

The inquest on the Thistle Hill body provided his wife with an opportunity to speak with authority about those events of long ago. At that time inquests were concluded before any murder trial began – unlike the modern system. The decision whether or not to prosecute a suspect was usually taken at the inquest, and so Anna Aram now found some willing listeners. Under questioning she confirmed that Daniel Clark had been a close friend of her husband's and that they had done business together many times before 8 February 1744–5, the precise year being lost to memory. Richard Houseman was often with them too.

Mrs Aram then told the coroner about the events of that fateful night.

She said that at about 6 p.m. her husband came home alone. She was washing in the kitchen, and Aram asked her to put out the downstairs fire and light one in one of the bedrooms. She did so and he went out. Then at 2 a.m. that morning, 8 February, Eugene returned with Clark and

Houseman. They went upstairs to the room where she had lit the fire, and Aram asked her for a handkerchief for Dickie (Richard Houseman). She lent him one and they left after about an hour. Clark was carrying a sack on his back. She had no idea where they went, but Aram and Houseman returned about 5 a.m. without Clark. Her husband came upstairs to ask for a candle because he wanted to light a fire downstairs; she objected, saying there was no need for two fires in the house. Aram said Dickie was staying downstairs, and this prompted her to ask about Daniel. Aram did not answer that question and told her to go to bed. He went down with the candle, and she then heard the two men talking about her, clearly worrying that she would tell someone about their deeds. She heard Aram tell Houseman not to worry, saying, 'We will coax her a little until her passion has worn off, and then take an opportunity to shoot her.' They then discussed what to do with her clothes, and this terrified her into remaining in her room until 7 a.m. Aram and Houseman had left a little earlier.

When she came down, she found the remains of a fire and remnants of burnt cloth and linen on the dunghill. She thought these were the remains of Clark's clothing. Then in the house she found the handkerchief she had lent Houseman. It was showing a patch of blood, about the size of a shilling. Later she asked them if they had harmed Clark, and each denied having hurt him.

The coroner examined several other witnesses, including Philip Coates, brother-in-law of Daniel Clark, and it became clear that the last people to be seen with Clark on 7 February were Eugene Aram and Richard Houseman.

Two doctors, a Mr Higgins and Mr Locock, both of Knaresborough, said they had examined the bones and, upon breaking the thigh bone, concluded the skeleton had been buried for about thirteen or fourteen years.

Richard Houseman was present at the inquest, and one old account says, 'He seemed very uneasy, revealing all the signs of guilt such as trembling, turning pale and faltering in his speech. This, with the strong circumstances given by Mrs Aram, gave a suspicion that he had been concerned in the murder of Clark, though he gave no account of the matter and denied that he knew anything concerning the matter.'

It was when the skeleton was produced at the inquest that Houseman made his famous remark – 'This is no more Dan Clark's bone than it is mine.'

The authorities thought that, if he was so sure that it was not Clark's bone, he must know what had happened to Clark. Under fierce questioning, Houseman then said he could produce a witness who had seen Clark two or three days after his alleged disappearance.

The witness, called Parkinson, was sent for but he was unclear as to whom he had seen. He said it had been snowing at the time, and the man he'd seen had had his coat collar turned up. Parkinson could not say who the man was.

Because there was suspicion that Houseman was implicated in the murder of Clark, the inquest decided that a warrant would be issued to apprehend Houseman and that depositions would be taken as a prelude to a trial at York Assizes.

This development terrified Houseman, who then said he would make a statement about the events of 7/8 February 1744–5. He admitted having been with Daniel Clark on the night he disappeared. He said he had earlier loaned Clark £20 and had met him to recover the loan, but Clark had given him some goods in lieu. It had taken some time to carry these from Clark's house to his own – there were leather and linen goods among them, and Clark had said that Houseman should sell them to recover his dues. Houseman then said he had left Clark at Aram's house, where there was another man; later Aram, Clark and that other man had left the house and followed Houseman to Knaresborough market-place. He did not know what happened afterwards and denied having gone to Aram's house as stated by Mrs Aram.

When asked to sign this statement, he refused, saying he might have something further to add. He was, however, committed to custody at York Castle on suspicion of having murdered Clark and was conveyed there by coach.

When passing through the village of Green Hammerton, Houseman indicated to his custodians that he knew something about the murder, and when descending Micklegate in York, they happened to see the magistrate, Mr Thornton, who, by chance, was passing by. Houseman asked Thornton if he could make a confession, and the magistrate agreed.

Houseman said that Daniel Clark had been murdered by Eugene Aram on Friday 8 February 1744–5. He gave an account of that night, saying there was snow on the ground, and admitted that the three of them had gathered at Aram's house. They then went out. It was now that Houseman produced the surprise: he said the body found at Thistle Hill was not that of Clark. Aram had struck Clark several times in an argument and Clark had fallen, as if dead. Houseman had then left the scene. He could not say whether Aram had used any weapon, nor could he say what had happened to the body, but later suggested it might have been hidden in St Robert's Cave near Grimbald Bridge, Knaresborough. He went further – he said the head of the body lay to the right in the turn at the entrance to the cave.

St Robert's Cave, which was close to the River Nidd, was searched and a skeleton was discovered lying in the position suggested by Houseman; medical evidence of the time showed that a blunt instrument had been driven into the bones of the skull, the resultant damage incapable of being the result of natural decay.

As a result of this, a warrant was issued for the arrest of Eugene Aram. He was found teaching at Lynn and brought back to Yorkshire for trial. He was examined by the local magistrate, Mr Thornton, and denied ever having been involved in any fraud and stated his complete innocence of murder.

Aram did not sign his first statement, saying he might wish to add further recollections, and later he did provide information about Clark's involvement with the fraudulent collection of plate and other goods, now implicating a licensee called Henry Terry who, said Aram, was involved in the fraud. Aram did admit having walked close to St Robert's Cave, where he had heard the sound of beating, but assumed it was Clark and Houseman beating some of the silverware to flatten it. Aram said he saw Houseman and Terry go into the cave; he never saw Clark but assumed he was there too. Terry was later indicted for fraud, but the magistrate felt there was sufficient evidence to commit both Aram and Houseman on a charge of having murdered Clark.

They appeared at York Assizes on 3 August 1759, whereupon Houseman, having turned King's Evidence, was acquitted. He gave evidence at the trial and said he had seen Aram strike Clark several times, whereupon he fell, never to rise again. The witnesses who had given evidence at the inquest were called and repeated their stories. The skull of the body found in St Robert's Cave was produced in court, to reveal a fracture on the left side, having apparently been caused by a blunt instrument.

Then it was the turn of Eugene Aram to speak in his own defence, and he produced a long, written statement which would have ensured his acquittal in a modern court. Although copies still exist, it is too lengthy to reproduce here in full.

He began with an account of his own character, saying he spent his time in learning and had never injured anyone. He mentioned his physical frailty, adding that he had once spent eighteen months in bed, enfeebled through distemper, and he asked the court to understand that he was too weak to have carried out the alleged murder.

But he went further. He claimed that the disappearance of Daniel Clark was not proof of his death. He added that many people had left the area without trace, and referred to a recent example, a local man who had also vanished in June 1757. He was called William Thompson. Then he produced his opinions about the discovered body.

No one had proved it was that of a male person, let alone that of Daniel Clark. He pointed out that the body had been found in a hermitage and added that in times past these were places of burial for holy men. In fact, the cave contains a stone coffin said to have been used by St Robert, and Aram told the judge of similar discoveries. He included the bones of the Saxon St Dubritius discovered in his cell at Guiscliffe near Warwick; the bones of a hermit called Rosia found at Royston in an undecayed state; the bones of hermit William of Lindholm, near Hatfield, found in 1747; some bones found at Woburn Abbey in February 1744 even with the flesh on, thought to have been there since the Dissolution of the Monasteries some 200 years earlier, and he referred to many others. He added that, at the Reformation many bodies of religious persons, alive and dead, had suffered injuries.

He provided examples of the difficulty of proving the identity of a dead person and added that, in his own case, two skeletons had already been discovered and none had been named. He gave examples where even the identity of living men had been difficult or impossible to establish.

Next he turned to the injury on the skull shown in court. He said that in May 1732 the body of William, the Lord Archbishop of York, was exhumed at York Minster and the bones of his skull were found to have been broken, and yet history confirmed he had not died by violence. Thus a fractured skull in a long-dead skeleton was not evidence of an attack.

He added that Knaresborough Castle had been besieged

many times and that no one really knew where the bodies of soldiers and others who had fallen were buried. Could not the body be such a relic? He mentioned several cases in which there had been errors of judgement and findings of guilt when innocence was later proved, and he referred in particular to a case in which two men called Harrison were thought to have murdered their lodger for his money. The lodger had disappeared and they were executed for the crime – then the lodger returned alive and well.

He said, 'As to the circumstances that have been raked together, I have nothing to observe, but that all circumstances whatsoever are precarious and have been frequently found lamentably fallible. My Lord,' he went on, 'I have endeavoured to show that the whole of this process is altogether repugnant to every part of my life … I put myself upon the candour, the justice, the humanity of your Lordship, and upon yours, my countrymen, gentlemen of the jury.'

But Eugene Aram's fine defence meant nothing to that judge or his jury. The judge, Mr Justice Bathurst, said Aram had alleged nothing to invalidate the positive evidence against him, nor had he done anything to counteract Houseman's damning story. Without leaving the court room, the jury found him guilty and he was sentenced to death.

While awaiting execution, it is said Aram admitted to two clergymen that he had murdered Clark, that he and Houseman had dragged the body into St Robert's Cave, stripped it of its clothes and burned them at Aram's house. He told the clergymen that he would make a further confession at his execution, but when the officers went in to fetch him to the gallows on York's Knavesmire, they found he had attempted suicide by cutting his wrists. But he survived that attempt and soon afterwards, as he mounted the scaffold, he was asked if he had anything further to say, and said, 'No.' His motive may have been the need for money, although he did believe that Clark was having an affaire with his wife. That motive never surfaced at his trial, and he is said to have confessed his suspicions about his wife to a priest before his death.

After his execution at York on 6 August 1759, his body was taken to Knaresborough Forest to be gibbeted – hung in chains to rot. The gibbet stood in the forest, to the south or south-west of Low Bridge and on the right-hand side of the road leading to Plompton. It was studded with nails to prevent people cutting it down, but when the forest was enclosed in 1778, the gibbet was removed. The skeleton had long since disappeared. The gibbet post, however, was installed at a Knaresborough inn, the Brewers Arms, formerly known as the Windmill Inn, where it served as a beam.

Afterwards Houseman married the widow of a man called Johnson; she had a daughter, Nancy, by her first husband. It was said that Houseman would rarely go out in the daytime. He tried several times to commit suicide by hanging himself from an apple tree, but his wife or her daughter Nancy always managed to cut him down before he died. It emerged later that after Clark's disappearance Houseman could often be seen wandering near St Robert's Cave and even creeping out of it, later to wash his hands in the river.

The cave was near the Low Bridge, along Abbey Road. The Trinitarian Priory of St Robert was built along here in around 1250; it followed the death of the saint who lived in his cave near Grimbald Bridge. The priory has now disappeared, but there remains the present Chapel of Our Lady of the Crag which was cut out of the rock around 1408 and which has more recently been restored. This is sometimes mistaken for St Robert's Cave, which was closer to the river, for the chapel has a mysterious figure guarding the entrance which is sometimes thought to be that of St Robert. It is probably one of the Knights Templar, for they had a training-ground nearby at Little Ribston.

The house in which Eugene Aram lived was up a passage in Vicarage Lane, Knaresborough, and afterwards it became a weaving shop. Vicarage Lane is just off Pump Hill at the foot of the High Street. The fireplace and bedroom mentioned at the trial remained for some twenty years after this conversion. Houseman's flax shop was over some stabling near White Horse Yard, and its back door emerged into the same yard as the school in which Aram taught, this later becoming a brewhouse. His school stood near the entrance of what is now Park Square, which leads off the High Street.

Although the name of Eugene Aram lives on in Knaresborough and although researchers will continue to debate his guilt, the strange case of Daniel Clark's death has left another mystery. Whose was the first body, the one found at Thistle Hill? A report at the time suggested it was also the victim of murder.

6 Mary Bateman of Leeds

Mary Bateman was an habitual fraudster. Modern society would describe her as a compulsive confidence trickster. Throughout her life she could never cease lying and cheating; even in the death cell, she tricked a fellow prisoner out of some money. For all her faults, she was frequently willing to admit her offences and often repaid those whom she had defrauded. But when she was convicted of murder, she stoutly denied that crime and then, before she was due to be executed, said she was pregnant. So was this yet another of Mary's lies, another of her many confidence tricks, or was she genuinely pregnant? Surely, she pleaded, the authorities would never hang a woman who was soon to have a child?

Mary was born in 1768. She was then Mary Harker, and her home was in the tiny North Yorkshire village of Topcliffe, near Thirsk.

Topcliffe lies in the huge Vale of Mowbray and is situated on a cliff which overlooks the River Swale as it meanders from Swaledale towards the North Sea via the Ouse and Humber. The village has its place in history. There is an impressive church whose origins date to the fourteenth century and which contains some magnificent brass, including a palimpsest bearing the oldest-known engraving of a ship on any brass in England.

An ancient castle stood here too. It was at Maiden Bower and was the home of William de Percy. This wooden fort was the first home of the Percy family, later to become earls of Northumberland, and part of the fabric of English society for generations. Among their number was 'Hotspur', alias Harry Percy, who was immortalized by William Shakespeare, and Richard Percy, a witness to the signing of the Magna Carta, who lived at Topcliffe.

Mary Harker was from more humble origins: her father was a farmer in a very modest way. From the outset Mary showed a remarkable ability for learning. She was able to read and write at an early age, but it seems she also developed a very low cunning. Her intelligence was directed towards making use of that cunning, and it seems she was never taught the difference between right and wrong. As a small girl, she started to steal and tell lies but was seldom corrected; instead, her actions were treated as jokes and a laughing matter, and so she grew bolder. Even as a child, she began to embezzle those around her, lying and cheating to gain small amounts of cash.

It seems that her father thought she would benefit from a change, and when she was thirteen he secured a post for her in Thirsk. She was to work in domestic service, and apparently for a while she did curb her thefts. There is no record of her being discharged for dishonesty at this time. But she decided to move to a bigger place.

When she was nineteen, she left Thirsk and obtained a job in York, and here she revealed her true nature. After working for a year in service for a dressmaker, who showed Mary a little of her craft, she was caught in an attempt to commit a robbery. But it seems she was not prosecuted. Instead she ran away, this time to Leeds. It was 1788 and she was now twenty. In Leeds she obtained work as a dressmaker, her speciality being mantuas (loose-fitting garments worn by the women of that time). But Mary's skills were not of a very high standard. She found herself producing cheap clothes rather than garments of any quality. Nonetheless, she worked in this way for the next four years. In the meantime she turned her skills towards earning extra cash. Whether or not she resorted to theft is not known, nor is it recorded whether or not she practised her confidence tricks, but she did begin to tell fortunes. There is little doubt that she abstracted hard-earned cash from people such as servants and that they boasted of Mary's fortune-telling ability to their young mistresses, who in turn paid Mary for her doubtful skills.

Then Mary became a bride. In 1792, when she was twenty-four, she married John Bateman. He was an honest man and a good, hard worker who had met her only three weeks earlier. It seems he had links with Thirsk, for his father was town crier there, and it also seems that Mary's silver tongue had charmed him into believing she was in love. They moved into lodgings in High Court Lane, Leeds.

It is felt that John Bateman had no idea of his wife's criminal tendencies, but once married and installed in their own home, Mary extended her fortune-telling enterprise. She included other activities, such as the removal of evil spells placed upon her customers by witches. She even said she could influence the future of her clients, but added that this was not something she accomplished alone. Mary claimed that the actual power came from a Mrs Moore who had supernatural skills because she was the seventh child of a seventh child; Mary claimed she was merely an agent of Mrs Moore. There is little doubt that 'Mrs Moore' was a figment of Mary's imagination, for she was to later make use of similar unseen helpers.

It was while at High Court Lane that Mary was caught stealing. From a lodger in the same house she stole a silver spoon, a silver watch and 2 guineas. When she was caught, Mary immediately confessed and made restitution, thus avoiding prosecution. She was also discovered stealing silk from various dressmakers' premises, but convinced the owners she was a poor girl and sought clemency – which they readily gave. From this stage, she increased her activities, often resorting to fraud.

When a neighbour's husband died, leaving his widow with four stepchildren, Mary told the widow that the eldest boy, aged fifteen, intended to sell everything and leave home. She advised the mother to sell up before the boy could achieve his aim and to quit Yorkshire, leaving a share for the children. The woman did as suggested and handed the children's share to Mary, for her to pass to the family. But Mary kept the money and turned the children over to the parish. Then she and John moved house, this time to Old Assembly Room Yard, off Kirkgate in the centre of Leeds.

While living here, she overheard a gentleman in a butcher's shop ask for a leg of mutton to be delivered to his home in Meadow Lane. She knew the butcher's boy would pass over a certain bridge and waited for him. She pretended she was the gentleman's servant, remonstrated with the boy for being late and took the meat from him, saying she would take it to the address herself. She took it home and began to cook it. But the gentleman returned to the butcher to ask about its non-delivery; the butcher had recognized Mary when she had been standing near the stall, and her description matched that of the woman who had taken the meat from the delivery boy. They all went to Mary's house and caught her roasting the joint. She apologized and paid for it, and so avoided another prosecution.

In 1793 the Batemans moved to a small house in Well's Yard, Leeds, and John furnished it from his hard-earned cash. But Mary now tricked *him*. She went to his place of work with a letter; she said it had come from his father in Thirsk, and that he was gravely ill. John rushed off to Thirsk and as he entered the town saw his father alive and well, in the act of announcing an auction in the market-place.

He went back to Leeds to tell Mary he'd been the victim of a hoax but found that every item of furniture had been stripped from his house. Mary had sold it to pay compensation to a victim of one of her robberies. It seems that John forgave his wife. To buy more furniture they took in lodgers, but Mary stole some money from one of them, a Mr Dixon; when she was found out, she repaid him and also reimbursed him for other losses while there.

By now, John Bateman had come to realize that his wife was a thoroughly bad woman and a notorious confidence trickster, thief and scoundrel. In 1796 he decided to join the army to get away from her – but she went with him. Thus she found a whole range of new victims who did not know of her reputation, and she exercised her formidable skills on them. But within a few months her activities led to John's being asked to leave, which he did. He came back to Leeds, and they lived in another house in Marsh Lane.

It seems Mary had no conscience. When a factory was destroyed by fire in 1796, several people losing their lives, she went around the town collecting linen sheets from generous householders. She said they were to help the victims' families but instead she pawned them. She also pretended she was a nurse from the general infirmary and collected old linen to dress the wounds of the injured. But she kept it for herself and sold it.

Her fortune-telling was still attracting clients, and she was still making use of the fictitious 'Mrs Moore'. Not all her attempts were successful, however. On one occasion she tried to convince a Mrs Greenwood that she, Mrs Greenwood, would soon commit suicide owing to her domestic problems. Mary knew that Mr Greenwood was working away from home but falsely claimed he had been arrested on a criminal charge and locked up. She said he was being guarded by four men. Mary said that, through the agency of Mrs Moore, she could immobilize those four guards and to allow Mr Greenwood to gain his freedom and come home to be with his wife. If this did not happen, said Mary, Mr Greenwood would be dead before morning, and at some future time Mrs Greenwood would kill herself. The terrified woman asked how all this could be prevented.

Mary said she needed four sheets of blotting-paper, four pieces of leather, four pieces of gold and four brass screws. These would be used in a charm which would 'screw down' the guards. Mrs Greenwood produced all these items except the pieces of gold, saying she had none. Mary then suggested she go out and borrow some or, if that failed, steal some. This last suggestion alerted Mrs Greenwood to the falsity of the plan and she refused to go ahead.

This failure did not deter Mary, for she tried a similar ruse upon another woman. She was a Mrs Stead, the wife of a man who had the unusual Christian name of Barzillai. He was a businessman, albeit not very successful, and he was also a member of the part-time army, the supplementary militia.

Mary had long been trying to harass Mr Stead, saying the bailiffs were always looking for him. She claimed she could ease his worries through the agency of Mrs Moore, but that any moneys earned thereafter would have to be shared with Mrs Moore. It seems she did have some success in convincing Mr Stead of her abilities, but then she turned her attentions to Mrs Stead. She decided to make her suspicious of her husband by suggesting he was having an affaire with a young woman who lived in Vicar Lane, Leeds. She told Mrs Stead that Barzillai was going off to camp with his part-time regiment and that this young woman intended going with him.

Mary claimed she could prevent this by screwing down the other woman, through the help of Mrs Moore. She said that Mrs Moore's screws would never operate without cash, and so she asked for three half-crowns and two pieces of coal. She would place the coal on the doorstep of the other woman's home, and when the woman discovered them, she would put them on her fire and this would cause her to fall into a deep sleep. The fire would burn brightly and the pieces of coal would fall out of the grate to destroy the clean clothes the woman had organized for her trip. Thus she would not be able to accompany Barzillai. All Mary needed to achieve this success was money, but Mrs Stead had none.

Mary said she would put the scheme into motion the moment Barzillai left to join his regiment, and perhaps the woman could sell something to raise the cash? This was agreed.

Mary therefore put the first part of the charm into operation – so she said. Barzillai left home as planned, albeit without the fictitious other woman, and Mary then persuaded Mrs Stead to sell several items of furniture to raise the necessary funds. But while her husband was away, Mrs Stead grew very depressed and suicidal, and so Mary persuaded her to sell more household goods to raise more cash to pay for more charms from the fictitious Mrs Moore.

In the end Mrs Stead, with no money and no furniture, did attempt suicide, and her plight reached the notice of the Leeds Benevolent Society. The society awarded her a guinea to ease her financial plight. It was a considerable sum at that time. The money was to be paid in three instalments each of 7 shillings, but the avaricious Mary managed to extort 8 shillings of this amount by claiming she could screw down the society to pay more!

Mary was not yet finished with Mrs Stead. The only thing she possessed were a few tools her husband had left upon joining the part-time army, and Mary said she should pawn these to raise even more money to 'screw down' the officers in her husband's regiment. If they were screwed down, said Mary, Barzillai would be free to come home. Mrs Stead parted with her cash, but her husband did not come home.

We are not told what eventually happened to the hapless Mrs Stead.

Having ruined this woman, Mary turned her attentions to the wife of another tradesman called Cooper. She managed to convince Mrs Cooper that her husband was on the point of absconding with all the family's money and goods and suggested that Mrs Cooper safeguard the belongings by storing them at the Bateman household. Mrs Cooper did so, and Mary Bateman pawned the lot.

Her next trick was perhaps her most famous. She and her long-suffering husband moved to yet another house, this time in Black Dog Yard, and there she kept a few hens. One day the neighbour was astounded to learn that one of Mary's hens had laid an egg bearing the words 'CHRIST IS COMING'. It was later revealed by Mary that the same hen had laid two more eggs bearing the same message, and she invited people to come and see this amazing bird. In fact, she hid some eggs beneath it so that they could be produced for inspection by unbelievers. And she charged everybody one penny for visiting her astonishing hen. She made a lot of money for this trick, and those who disbelieved the truth of the miracle were castigated by those who believed it was a genuine sign from God.

No one is quite sure why Mary had apparently become rather religious, although it was rumoured that she had fallen under the influence of another extraordinary woman, Joanna Southcote, a religious maniac who made many bizarre prophecies and who had gained a huge following. One of her claims was that she was to be the mother of the new Messiah. He was never born, and Joanna died in 1814, aged sixty-four.

Mary's activities had now reached a more sinister level. Just after the turn of the nineteenth century, she somehow ingratiated herself with two spinster ladies called Kitchin. They were sisters and they were Quakers, very honest and trustworthy ladies who ran a small linen and draper's shop near St Peter's Square in Leeds. It seems Mary convinced them that she knew something of dress-making, but she also persuaded them that she could foretell their futures. Thus she became a trusted confidante of the sisters.

In September 1803 one of the sisters became very ill. She was given medicines prescribed by Mary Bateman, who said she obtained them from a good country doctor, and so Mary continued with her treatment. Within a week this Miss Kitchin died. Mrs Kitchin, who lived in Wakefield, rushed to be with her daughter but was too late; nonetheless, she remained in the house with her surviving daughter, who also became ill. And then the mother became ill. Both had used Mary's medicines. Within ten days both were dead.

It was said they had died of cholera, but Mary did not accept this. She told everyone they had died of the plague, which meant that all the neighbours kept as far as possible away from the Kitchins' house. Mary remained at the house, some thinking she was heroic in not taking the risk of spreading the plague to those outside, and then, after the triple funeral, she left and the house and shop were locked.

Meanwhile a doctor had expressed some alarm about the circumstances of the three deaths. He did express a belief that the women could have been poisoned and asked to examine various bottles and containers in the house; one of his questions was whether any water kept for killing flies had been used. He did know that all the medicines had been administered by Mary Bateman and that she alone had given food to the women. But as the family had been wiped out, there was no one to give support to the doctor when he said he wanted to carry out a post mortem on at least one of the victims. Because no one would support him, no medical examination was conducted and so the funerals went ahead.

Later, when creditors came to examine the shop, the house and their contents, everything had been stripped bare. The shop's goods had been raided, the contents of the house removed and even the shop's books and records taken.

Mary had escaped justice once again, but continued

with her nefarious activities. She persuaded two servant girls to rob their mother of various items, including a family Bible, and then suggested they go to live in Manchester where a charm would be effected which would be of great benefit. If the charm was to work, Mary told them, they must never speak to one another.

When they arrived at Manchester, Mary wrote to each girl, asking them to send clothes to her. And so they did. They sent Mary clothes and money in the belief that these acts were essential to the working of Mary's charm. When by chance they met in the streets, each now destitute, the truth of the hoax emerged and they contacted their family, who then forced Mary to repay everything she had stolen from them.

Mary was now becoming more dangerous because, in her role as a witch and adviser, she had access to poisons. She made good use of poison in a further hoax. She discovered a girl who believed she had been subjected to an evil curse by an old beggar-woman. Mary said she could cure the girl and that she would consult an expert on these matters, a Miss Blythe. Miss Blythe was another figment of Mary's imagination, just like the earlier Mrs Moore. Mary said that Miss Blythe required £5 and some clothing to the same value. These items would be placed in bags and retained by Miss Blythe until the curse had been removed, whereupon they would be restored to the owner. Mary, of course, would see that Miss Blythe received them.

This part of the hoax achieved, a visitor arrived with a fruit pie for the girl and said that it had come from the person who would be her sweetheart. The girl tasted it; it was terrible. She made a servant taste it too, and she found it inedible. Wondering if something was wrong with the pie, the girl went to find Mary. Mary examined it and said it contained poison, adding that, if she had eaten the whole pie, she would have died. Thus Mary's reputation was enhanced and her prophecy was true – the charm had saved the girl from the evil curse of the old beggar-woman. This done, it was now time to open the bags kept by the supposed Miss Blythe, but the money had gone and the clothes had turned into rags.

It seems now that Mary's infamous conduct was becoming known to the citizens of Leeds, and she had to move house yet again, this time to premises in Meadow Lane. A near neighbour was a man called Joseph Gosling, and he had a family of four small children. He was very poor, and life was a struggle, but he did love his family and often took them on outings. Mary, appears to have resented the boisterous playing of the children and complained about the noise. Then one day when they returned home, the 7-year-old boy noticed a cake on the table, and he, his mother and the other children shared it. All were violently sick and a doctor had to be called. He saved their lives by his quick action and decided to examine the remains of the cake. It was found to contain arsenic. No one knew who had placed the cake on the family table, and although Mary fell under suspicion, she was not prosecuted.

Later, in April 1807, an old washerwoman called Judith Cryer became worried about the behaviour of her 11-year-old grandson, and someone suggested Mary Bateman could help. Mrs Cryer therefore went to see Mary and asked if she could find a way of making the boy behave himself. Mary said she would seek the advice of her friend, Miss Blythe. She told Judith Cryer that Miss Blythe lived at Scarborough and said she would write to her.

A few days later Mary said a letter had arrived from Miss Blythe – it contained a drawing of a gallows with a rope dangling from it. The letter went on to say that when the boy was fourteen he would be hanged. This horrified Judith Cryer, but Mary raised her hopes by saying that his salvation could be arranged for the sum of 4 guineas, which must be handed to Miss Blythe. For the old lady, this was an enormous sum, but she did find it and handed it to Mary Bateman; Mary said she would keep it until the charm had succeeded. Eventually 'Miss Blythe' wrote to say that 3 guineas must be put into a leather container and sewn into Judith Cryer's bed. It must remain untouched until the boy's fourteenth birthday. This was duly done. Later, when Mary was arrested for another crime, Judith opened the bag sewn into her bed and it was empty.

The following year the Batemans moved yet again, this time to Camp Field in Water Lane, Leeds. It was now 1808, and Mary found another victim. The wife of James Snowdon, a near neighbour, feared that one of her children would be drowned. It seems she had received some kind of premonition and was sure that this would shortly occur. Mary learned of her fears and offered to help save the child. She said that her friend Miss Blythe, who now lived in Thirsk, could offer a solution, and in due course a letter was supposedly received from Miss Blythe which said that Mr Snowdon's silver watch must be sewn into his bed by Mary Bateman. This was done. After a while, another letter arrived, this time asking for 12 guineas which Mary had also to sew into the bed. Mary said these items would be restored once the charm had succeeded in its aims, but then she said she had received information from Miss Blythe that, unless the family moved from Leeds to Bradford, the daughter would suffer a fatal attack of some kind. Frightened by this news, the Snowdons agreed and packed their belongings. Mary said they could take the bed and its valuable contents, but they did leave some items behind and allowed Mary to have the key. They moved to Bowling, near Bradford.

Later they contacted Mary and said they wished to remove the money and the watch from the bed, but Mary persuaded them to leave it, as the right time had not yet arrived. They consented – Mary said the charm was expected to reach its climax in October that year, 1808. She would be in touch before then.

What in fact she did was to prepare a poisonous dose for them. This would prevent their discovering her hoax and contacting the authorities. But fate was on their side. Before Mary could administer that dose, possibly due to the distance involved, she was arrested for a series of frauds that had occurred a couple of years earlier.

Her victims then had been a family called Perigo. They were poor but trusting and lived at Armley, near Leeds. Mary had convinced Mrs Perigo that she could absolve her from the effects of an evil wish and, exercising her usual trickery and deceit, managed to relieve the family of over £70 in cash. As with previous cases, she had pretended to sew the money into the bedding, on the understanding that it would be returned to the family when the spell had succeeded. The spell, operated from a distance by 'Miss Blythe', would ensure that Mrs Perigo was relieved from the mental burden which plagued her life. As with the case of the Snowdons, Mary said that the spell would be activated on a certain date, after which the cash would be restored. But before that date arrived, she fed the Perigos with poisoned food. Mrs Perigo died, but her husband recovered. He was able to give an account of the events which had led to the death of his wife on 24 May 1806, more than two years before Mary's arrest for the crime of murder.

When Mary felt that she was to be exposed, Mr Perigo began to receive letters from 'Miss Blythe', one of which stated that he had been told not to allow his wife to eat the things which eventually caused her death. The letter said that Miss Blythe herself, when at Scarborough, had nearly died through eating the same food, and so had Mary Bateman of Leeds ... The letter went on to say that Mrs Perigo would rise from her grave and stroke his face with her right hand, after which he would lose the movement of that side of his face.

On 19 October 1808 William Perigo ripped open the bed in which the family cash had been placed by Mary

Bateman, and found no cash at all. There was some waste paper and a halfpenny or a farthing, but no large sums. He wasted no time in confronting Mary with his suspicions, but she simply said, 'The time was not ready, you opened the bed too soon.' But he replied, 'I think it is too late.'

Perigo then threatened Mary. He said he would return to her house with two or three men to sort out the problem. Mary pleaded with him to wait. She asked for a meeting at a place where they could be alone; she said he could appoint the time and the place. He selected a point on the Leeds–Liverpool Canal near a bridge in Leeds, and she agreed. The date was determined as 21 October 1808.

But two officers of justice were also waiting; they had heard Perigo's story and arrested Mary, on a charge not only of fraud but also of murdering Mrs Rebecca Perigo of Bramley.

Mary was remanded in custody at York Castle to await the next assizes. By now she had a small daughter of only ten months, and the child was placed beside her in the cell.

The judge was Sir Simon Le Blanc, and the trial began on 17 March 1809.

The evidence so carefully gathered about this extraordinary criminal was such that the court had no difficulty in finding Mary guilty of all charges, and she was condemned to death. She was forty-one years old.

But Mary now produced yet another trick. She told the judge that she was pregnant. When she made this announcement, there was a stampede to leave court. The stampede comprised ladies from the public gallery, because they suddenly realized that twelve of them would be required to examine Mary Bateman and that they would be responsible for deciding whether or not she was telling the truth.

None wanted that responsibility. But the judge was just as quick – he ordered that all doors be locked, and so he secured twelve 'volunteers'. They adjourned with Mary, and examined her, then returned to the court to pronounce that, in their opinion, she was not pregnant. (If she had been, the duration of that pregnancy would have been important. A woman less than 4½ months pregnant could be executed, whereas anyone more than 4½ months pregnant would not be executed until after the birth. After the child had been born, the sentence would be carried out.) So this trick did not work.

As Mary awaited execution, the Revd George Brown asked her to make a full confession and reminded her about other deaths of which there was suspicion against her. In particular he referred to the Misses Kitchin, the two Quakers. But Mary denied all guilt. Throughout her time in the death cell, she persisted on her innocence of any murder. But even in these circumstances she could not resist yet another fraud, and even this was not her final money-making enterprise.

When a fellow prisoner, a young girl, expressed a wish to see her sweetheart, Mary said she could arrange it. She needed some money to effect the necessary charm. It would be sewn into the girl's clothing close to her breast, and this would compel the boyfriend to visit her. The girl produced some money, and Mary bound it in cloth and sewed it close to the girl's breasts. But no sweetheart came – and when the girl opened the charm, there was no money inside. Mary had done it again.

On the day before her execution, she wrote to her faithful and long-suffering husband and expressed sincere regret at the disgrace she had brought to him and her young daughter. In that letter, she insisted she was innocent of murder and sent her wedding ring to him with the request that he keep it for their little girl.

The time of her execution was noon on Monday 20 March 1809. At 5 a.m. she was removed from her cell without awakening her child, who slept at her side; Mary halted and kissed her but showed no emotion at leaving the child and even at that late stage refused to confess to murder, in spite of pleas from her chaplain. At noon Mary Bateman was executed.

Her body was taken to the general infirmary in Leeds, where it was exhibited at a charge of 3 pence per person, the income thus generated being used for the benefit of the hospital. 2,500 people queued to see the body of this notorious woman, and more than £30 was raised. Mary had done well in her final fund-raising triumph.

Later her body was dissected for medical research and, in accordance with a curious Yorkshire custom of the time, portions of her skin were tanned and distributed to those who applied for it. Thus pieces of Mary Bateman were spread around Leeds, but her skeleton is still on show in the Medical School. Mary Bateman is by no means forgotten.

7   Corpses and Caves

Some of Yorkshire's most spectacular scenery lies underground in a network of massive caves. Most of them are beneath the higher points of the Pennines, although others are located elsewhere within the county. Deep within these caves, there are cliffs, lakes, waterfalls, rivers and beautifully created designs in stalagmites and stalactites. No one is quite sure how many caves lie undiscovered, for new entrances and new networks, large and small, are regularly found, often by accident, and the area has been described as a vast underground honeycomb of passages and chambers. The Yorkshire Dales are home to Britain's premier pot-holing region – 'pot-holing' being the name given to exploration of these caves by means of such aids as ladders, ropes, torches and radios.

New caves continue to be found. In 1975, for example, some workmen on a farm near Arncliffe in Littondale discovered a hitherto-unknown underground system which ran beneath the kitchen of the farmhouse. The cave was over a mile long, with several passages and so a whole new caving system was registered. It was called 'Robinson Pot' after the brothers who farmed above it, and it confirmed a legend which had circulated for years. People said that if you stood at a certain place in Littondale, you could hear the Robinsons poking their kitchen fire. Those underground passages might well have provided the necessary sound-relay system.

In another case, a farm between Lofthouse and Middlesmoor sits over the River Nidd as it flows underground, and in times of flood the noise of the river had been heard by anyone above ground. In October 1892 it flowed so near the surface that it bubbled up through a fireplace in someone's living-room.

In addition to natural caves, Yorkshire has countless man-made excavations such as old mine workings, whether for lead, coal or iron ore, and there are huge hollows in the earth, such as the famous Buttertubs on the road between Hawes and Muker. Old wells and pits which have served varying purposes can be added to this assortment of subterranean hollows and chambers.

Some of the larger caves have been adapted for entry by the public, such as Stump Cross Cavern between Grassington and Pateley Bridge. This was discovered accidentally around 1850 by a lead-miner, and it is now equipped with electric lights, gravel paths and a visitor centre complete with shop and café.

The Stump Cross complex can be explored in safety and comfort, but a visit to Gaping Ghyll, discovered in 1895, remains something of an adventure. The first descent was by a Frenchman called Martel, who used a rope ladder with a lantern fastened to his arm. Now, by courtesy of the local caving club, gallant visitors can be winched down in a bosun's chair type of apparatus, and thus they can gain some experience of England's largest underground cavern. It is over eighty feet high and more than 500 feet long and is large enough to contain York Minster. It costs nothing to enter this impressive place – but you have to pay to get out!

Many of the less commercialized caves require a dedication that is extraordinary. Exploration is by crawling on hands and knees along dark, narrow passages, often immersed in dirty water or mud, and sometimes not knowing whether there is any exit. This sport is exciting but it is highly dangerous, especially to the unskilled. One of the chief risks comes from a sudden shower of rain on the surface. Quite suddenly, this can produce rushing rivers of floodwater deep within a cave, and deaths have resulted from this source.

The worst disaster of this kind occurred at Mossdale Caverns near Grassington in 1967. On Saturday 14 July ten cavers squeezed through the narrow entrance to explore the three miles or more of very dirty, wet and dark passages. The day was grey and there was some drizzle, but as the cavers worked their way deep inside the hill, the drizzle became rain. Many of these caves serve as drains for the surrounding fells, and as the moorland above Mossdale Caverns became awash, so the floodwaters found their way into this cave.

Four of the cavers emerged late in the afternoon and left their six companions behind, not realizing that tragedy was about to envelope them. It was later that same evening that the full horror was appreciated, when the entire entrance was completely submerged and the rain continued to pour down. No one could enter the cave to attempt a rescue. Not until the following day could entry be made, and then only with great risks to the rescuers. Five bodies were found. It was several more days before the sixth was discovered, and it was impossible to remove the bodies from the cave.

With the consent of the coroner, the bodies were left in the cave, and it was sealed to become their tomb. Later, however, friends of the six deceased cavers were allowed inside to bury their colleagues in a high-level chamber at the end of this caving system. They lie there today.

Although many deaths in caving have occurred through drowning as a result of flooding, other cavers have become trapped, to die of hypothermia and exhaustion, while yet more have survived falls or being trapped with such injuries as broken limbs and severe bruising. A woman died in July 1936 when a stone was recklessly thrown down Alum Pot, and in 1955 a pot-holer fell from his rope ladder and was killed.

In all cases, rescue is extremely difficult – one man was trapped for 8½ hours in a passage only eight inches high, and it is not unknown for rescuers deliberately to break a man's ribs in order to effect his rescue.

Unless one knows these caverns well, they could be thought ideal hiding-places for murder victims, but in truth it would be the most difficult of tasks to manoeuvre a corpse into these narrow passages. Besides, with the rapid expansion of interest in caving since the 1960s, a corpse in such a hiding-place is almost certain to be discovered.

These caves are not friendly places, and it is almost certain that ancient man has not lived in all of them. Their inner passages are so difficult to negotiate and are simply too dark, too wet, too dangerous and virtually impossible to colonize as domestic dwelling-places, although there are exceptions.

Some *have* been used as dwellings. Victoria Cave, near Settle, and Kinsey Cave, near Giggleswick, are known to have been occupied by prehistoric people around 9000 BC, for ivory tools, flints and other implements have been found there. Embolton Cave near Grassington was colonized around 3000 BC, but it seems the dead were buried on the surface in barrows. At Tom Taylor's Cave, near Brimham Rocks, some Roman coins were discovered in 1868 and dated to the time of Septimius Severus (AD 197–211): this cave was once the haunt of an outlaw. Not far away is the mysterious Eglin's Hole, which extends for almost two miles into the hillside. The massive Yordas Cave near Ingleborough was said to be the dwelling-place of a giant called Yordas, although the name is said to have come from ancient Norse words meaning 'Earth-House Cave' that is, *iord* (earth) and *hus* (house).

Local folk-memory, or perhaps a hint of folklore, hints that a queen once lived in a Yorkshire cave near Malham, when she needed somewhere to hide from her enemies; but dates and names are lacking. Another story of the same cave is that it sheltered members of an invading

Scottish army. They stayed overnight following one of their forays to the south, probably to Derby, and the local people were astonished by the sight of men in petticoats who talked in an incomprehensible language. Skulls were found in the nearby bogs, as if some battle or slaughter had occurred. But it is all vague folk-memory.

Years ago some bones of children were found in one cave. This was Dowka Bottom Cave near Kilnsey. Situated almost a thousand feet above sea-level, the cave centres upon a deep cavity from which narrow passages extend into the hillside. It has not been revealed how long those remains were in this cave; the remains of several adults have also been found here, as well as those of animals which have been long extinct in Britain. The most astonishing find here, around 1860, was beneath the base of a stalagmite that had fractured; it was a basalt adze of a kind found previously only in New Zealand.

Animal remains dating back thousands of years have also been discovered in some caves. The remains of wolverines and hyenas have been discovered in Stump Cross Cavern, while Victoria Cave near Settle yielded a mass of information. Discovered in 1838, Queen Victoria's coronation year, by a Settle man whose dog squeezed through a narrow gap, this cave is almost 1,500 feet above sea-level. The finds inside included bones of pre-glacial animals in the lower cave, Mesolithic Age implements in the middle cave, and Iron Age relics in the upper cave. That man had lived here was clearly shown by such objects as a harpoon, some Roman coins and a brooch over 2,000 years old. But this cave had also been the haunt of animals normally found only in a tropical climate, such as hyenas, elephants, rhinoceros and hippopotamus. Once this area did enjoy such a climate but the cave also showed relics of the Ice Age such as the bones of bear and reindeer. It seems the hyenas hunted other species and brought their remains here for their meals.

In 1821 similar discoveries were made in Kirkdale Cave

on the edge of the North York Moors. Finds there match those of Victoria Cave, for the bones came from both the warm and cold periods and included those of the wolf, fox, brown bear, cave bear, stoat, lion, spotted hyena, mouse, water vole, Abbot's vole, short-tailed field vole, brown hare, rabbit, slender-nosed rhinoceros, woolly rhinoceros, horse, pig, reindeer, hippopotamus, red deer, giant deer, European bison, wild ox, straight-toothed elephant and mammoth. These were dated as being relics of 70,000 years before Christ, but no human relics were found in that cave. It is possible that many unknown caving systems await discovery, but it is equally possible that some of the existing ones have been used, where possible, for the disposal of the evidence of murder or even as scenes of murder. Rumours have long abounded of people mysteriously disappearing, with tales of their being pushed or hidden within some of these caves or pits. To conceal a body in a cave would be difficult, because the body itself is too cumbersome to be manoeuvrable, but to cast it down a pit might be easy. Tales of hidden murder victims in these caves are a mixture of legend and fact, and at times it is not easy to distinguish one from the other.

Such a mystery surrounds the aptly named Troller's Gill near Appletreewick. This is more of a gorge than a cave, but it extends for about half a mile through limestone crags which are rich with caves and old mines. It is only a few yards wide at its broadest part, its rocks rising to some sixty feet. The stream which races through it, Skyreholme Beck, produces a terrifying roaring sound, and there is little wonder that the place has given rise to ghost stories and horror tales.

One legend suggests that a man met an awful death here, and this is supported by the legend of a barguest which haunts the area. A barguest was a ghostly hound with huge eyes and feet that left no marks on the ground and was distinguished by its ghastly howling. The name comes from *'berg-geist'* which means 'spirit of the bier' or 'mountain demon'. Some assumed the shape of other animals, such as calves, pigs, sheep, cats or even large rabbits. Sometimes they were said to be the ghosts of living creatures which had been buried within the foundations of new buildings. (This was a custom of the past which was said to strengthen the structure.)

If a barguest made an appearance, it was said to herald the death of a local person. In the case of Troller's Gill, the victim was a man called either Troller or Trowler, but the circumstances of his death are shrouded in mystery. Nonetheless, superstitious cavers and hikers keep well clear of Troller's Gill.

Another ghost haunts Stump Cross Caverns. This one wears clogs. From time to time witnesses tell of ghostly footsteps which echo in the sound of clogs, and in each case no one is to be seen. This was lead-mining country and the workers did wear clogs, so was one of them killed and buried in this cave? Certainly many of the caves have their own boggarts – ghostly apparitions. Hurtle Pot's boggart would drown people in a pool, for example, and one can only ponder at such names as Death's Head Hole, Lost Johns and Batty Wife Hole.

But both Trow Ghyll and Gaping Ghyll have produced fairly recent mysteries tinged initially with a suggestion of murder. Two skeletons were found in the summer of 1947, one in each cave, and because they were so close together and both lying within this caving system, a major inquiry was instituted. Both were male skeletons. Could these be two murder victims? Or a murder followed by a suicide?

In the case of Trow Ghyll, some pot-holers had been working on plans of the underground system when they came upon some bones. At first they thought these were the remains of a sheep or even a cow which had entered the cave and got lost, but a closer look at the skull showed that it was probably human. A leg bone added confirmation to this probability. These bones were brought to the surface. Officers of the West Riding Constabulary were notified, and their experts examined the remains. A forensic pathologist, asked to give his opinion, confirmed that the bones were human. Among the coins found near the site of the discovery, none was dated before 1944. Thus it seemed the body could have been there for two or three years, and in the opinion of the pathologist this was a case of suicide.

The second skeleton, found in Gaping Ghyll, lay on a ledge in the Great Chamber, the hole which is large enough to accommodate York Minster, and it was some thirty feet from the ground. No head was found but the legs had been thrust high into the trunk of the body, suggesting a fall from a very high place. The victim had landed on his feet, thus causing this terrible impacted injury.

In considering the coincidences presented by these two discoveries, the police and the pathologist wondered whether one had committed suicide having murdered the other, but further possibilities did present themselves.

As Gaping Ghyll was open with few, if any, restrictions on access, it was quite possible for a wanderer to venture too close to the opening and fall down; it was a sheer drop, and death would be inevitable.

Because of the date of the discoveries (1947), possible war casualties were also considered, perhaps servicemen lost during exercises on the fells or even from an aircraft crash or parachute drop. But no servicemen had been reported missing, and no plane crashes had occurred within that locality, although some had been reported on other Yorkshire fells.

It was felt almost certain that the Gaping Ghyll skeleton had not been there a year earlier, because the complex had been carefully explored by members of the British Speleological Association and they had not found any bones.

Although no firm conclusion could be reached, because

of the state of the skeletons, it was felt that the Trow Ghyll remains were the outcome of suicide, while those in Gaping Ghyll could also be the result of a suicide, but more probably death had occurred due to an accidental fall from a great height. In this case, the absence of the head could be explained by frequent flooding of the cave – whenever the cave was flooded, the body would have floated around. In the strong flow, pieces could have been torn off to be washed away. It is possible that the skull might, one day, be found.

In neither case was there any evidence or proof of murder, but in reaching their decision the experts failed to solve two further mysteries. Who were these men? No one was reported missing, and their identities have never been established.

Another story concerns the mass of disused lead mines on the moors around Yarnbury near Grassington. It is said that two bodies lie buried in Dowsyke Ghyll mine, but the passage of time has blurred the distinction between truth and legend.

In the area around Yarnbury, which features in the Tom Lee murder story (Chapter 2), there are scores of ancient workings, for during the seventeenth, eighteenth and nineteenth centuries this was a major lead-mining district. During that time Grassington, then known as 'Girston', was a prominent lead-mining town, the focal point of the Dales lead-mining industry.

Dowsyke Ghyll mine had been worked for many years, albeit in short bursts of activity which fluctuated with the rise and fall of lead prices. If the price was high, the men would attempt to glean more ore from Dowsyke: if the price was low, the effort was not worthwhile. There was a legend surrounding Dowsyke Ghyll. Local folklore said that a very rich seam of ore lay deep within this mine but that all attempts to reach it had failed. On one occasion, a pair of miners had actually succeeded in reaching the seam, but their work had brought down the roof and they had been trapped. According to local folklore, they lie here today, for no one could find them or their rich seam of ore.

This is the story. During the early days of mining here, some of the miners worked freelance. These were called 'adventurers', for they had to locate their own seams of ore and pay their own costs of abstracting and smelting it. Their income came from the sale of their lead. Clearly the discovery of a rich seam which could be easily and cheaply worked was a bonus.

One such team of adventurers comprised four local men. One of them was called Seth – his surname has been lost in the telling of this tale. Seth was a secretive man, although he was a very skilled tradesman and knew all there was to know about lead mining in and around Grassington. There were few to equal him in skill and knowledge. In reality, however, many of these characters never went to work on Mondays: they would avoid Mondays after an enjoyable break over the weekend, and so it was with Seth's team-mates. Seth was more ambitious, and he was prepared to work, but he could not achieve any great results without the assistance of his three companions. With his Mondays free, therefore, he decided to hunt the legendary bed of rich ore in Dowsyke Ghyll mine. If he found it, he knew he would have to reveal the secret to his pals. Operating alone, he would not be able to abstract and process the ore. But if he did find it, the profits would be sufficient for them all to be secure for a long, long time.

Each Monday, therefore, Seth began to explore the old mine workings. There were many abandoned levels, and he adopted a systematic plan to search every one. The various levels were linked with 'rises' (vertical shafts). He knew some of these because he and his team had worked here from time to time. But some of the rises had become blocked with fallen earth and rock, and some of the levels had also been lost.

To search this dirty, dark and disused old pit

thoroughly was far from easy, especially with such limited equipment, but Seth did not give up. In time his explorations became known to the others, and they all laughed at him. Surely, they chuckled, he did not believe in the old tale of the hidden seam? But Seth ignored them and worked on for weeks and weeks.

Then he found a tiny opening. It had been man-made; he recognized the indications and enlarged the hole, eventually crawling through to find a terrible fall of rock. This was new territory even for him, and in his heart of hearts he knew he had found the legendary fall. But what of the seam?

He had to remove all the fallen rock and earth, shore up the roof and make his own passage safe. There were some props which he could use – more evidence of the truth behind the story – and he worked on. It took him weeks to remove enough debris to provide a route.

Eventually he was able to crawl along and was delighted to find that he was upon a hitherto unknown level. He moved precariously in the darkness, his only light coming from the lantern he carried, and as his hand reached out ahead to feel the way, he came upon some clothing. For a moment he was horrified, but then his lantern picked out a body. It was a human body which had been reduced to bones, although its clothing was intact. So the legend was true. But there was only one body here. The stories said there was a second one.

Seth did not try to find the second. Instead, he knew he was about to discover the legendary seam, and that was his dream. He inched his way forward, the light of his lantern picking out the ancient walls, the rotting timber props and the marks of earlier generations of lead miners. There were some abandoned tools too. And then the light of his lantern located the thick seam of lead ore, known as galena. It was a huge seam, at least six inches deep …

So the tales had been right! Generations of lead miners had told of this mystical seam, and he was the one who had found it! All that remained was to abstract it, then he and his three mates would be rich.

But he would have to convince them of his find, and so, by using one of the old abandoned picks, he decided to chip out some of the ore and show it to them. But as he worked, there was the ominous fall of dust, the rumble of rocks somewhere above …

Within seconds the entire roof had caved in and Seth was trapped. He had no air … his only chance of survival was to remove the debris, but it would take days … Desperately he started to dig his way to freedom, but it was impossible. There was too much debris and too little time; he worked as only a man of his skill could, but he was not to succeed. And as he gradually sank into oblivion, he knew that, after all, the legend was true.

There *was* a rich seam of ore and there *were* two bodies in Dowsyke Ghyll mine – or there would be when the next adventurer came this way.

Another case involves a pit shaft at Walton, near Wakefield in West Yorkshire.

In 1942, during the early days of the Second World War, an elderly lady vanished from her home in Chevet Terrace. Her name was Emma Sheard, and she was seventy-five years old. She lived at that address with her great-niece, who was a nursing orderly. The younger woman was married, and her name was Winifred Hallaghan.

When the neighbours began to ask Winifred what had happened to her great-aunt, they were told she had gone away for a while, and as time went by without any trace of the old lady, her mysterious disappearance was almost forgotten. A year or so later, however it seemed that Emma Sheard was alive and well, because she sold her own cottage, and the conveyance of sale bore her signature. But almost seven years after her disappearance, the truth of Emma Sheard's fate was to make itself known.

Not far away from Winifred Hallaghan's terrace house was a disused pit shaft. It was at the other side of the road, within sight of her home. It was surrounded by wooden railings, and the old winding-gear was still in position. The top of the open shaft had been covered with stout boarding to prevent anyone from accidentally falling down.

Over the years of disuse, the shaft had become flooded. Some seventy years earlier, the pit shaft had led to the underground workings of this old pit, but when the floodwaters entered the mine, the entire complex had been abandoned. All the Victorian machinery and other equipment had been left underground. The pit shaft, like a huge well, contained 600 feet of water and this reached to within 130 feet of the top. The pit was therefore some 730 feet deep.

From time to time these old pit shafts were subject to examination by the coal-mining authorities, but the war had interrupted that inspection schedule. Thus several years had elapsed since Walton pit's last inspection. Once the war was over, the system was reinstated and the examinations were resumed. On the morning of 20 December 1948, therefore, a mining official came to inspect the old shaft at Walton.

He removed the covers and peered down into the water some 130 feet below. To his astonishment and horror, he saw something terrifying. Floating upon the surface of the stagnant water were what appeared to be the remains of a human body; even with his powerful lights, it was not easy to be sure that they were indeed human remains, but it was enough to raise his suspicions, and so he called the police.

Officers from the West Riding Constabulary came to the scene and began a routine examination. They were equipped with powerful lights and grappling-irons and, after initial searches around the scene, they attempted to raise the remains to the surface. They were successful and found that it was indeed a human body, but the head, forearms and one leg were missing. At this stage the remains were little more than a skeleton, and it was almost impossible to determine whether the body was male or female or to give any indication of its age.

The remains were taken to the Home Office pathological laboratory at Wakefield. There the pathologist, Dr David Price, carried out his careful examination and confirmed that the remains were those of a woman who, when living, would have been around five feet tall. He suggested the body had been in the water for a very long time – several years, in fact – but he was not able to determine the cause of her death, nor give any indications of a possible identity. Clearly, he said, it would be advantageous to recover the head if possible.

The police reasoned that the head had become detached from the skeleton through its immersion in water and had probably sunk to the bottom of the pit, a fate which had also occurred to the missing limbs. The problems of searching such a deep pit full of water were enormous – all sorts of other rubbish and debris would be at the bottom of the mine, along with mud and other unknown objects. But the skills of the mine rescue service were sought. With the aid of specially constructed equipment, including a cradle which made use of the surviving winding equipment, a mine rescue worker was lowered to the surface of the water. He was wearing protective clothing and equipped with an oxygen supply as he searched the deep water with his sophisticated equipment. In time the remains were recovered from the bottom of that pit. Every missing part was found.

As this lengthy and difficult task was being undertaken, the memories of the people of Walton were being revived, and as the police began their house-to-house enquiries in an effort to establish whether anyone had disappeared, it was recalled that Emma Sheard had vanished almost seven years earlier.

Her great-niece, Winifred Hallaghan, had not reported her disappearance to the police because she had not then been worried – indeed, her great-aunt was surely alive, for, as Winifred pointed out, she had sold her own house a year after she had left Walton. But police enquiries soon showed that there was no trace of the old lady; no one had seen her for years, and every enquiry led back to Winifred Hallaghan's house at Walton. The old lady had come to stay with her, and it was quickly evident that Winifred Hallaghan was lying.

Faced with intense pressure upon her conscience, Winifred soon confessed. After she had lived with her secret for seven years, the activities around the pit shaft so close to her home must have caused immense anxiety, apart from the fact that each time she left her home she would see the pit shaft and recall the fate of poor Great-aunt Emma. Winifred admitted having killed her great-aunt but denied having murdered her.

She claimed that there had been a fight between her and the old lady. During the latter days of the war, when the blackout was still being enforced, there was clearly some antagonism between the old lady and Winifred, with whom she was then living. Things came to a head when Emma Sheard told Winifred that her husband was seeing another woman. Winifred's response had been swift – she had hit out at the old lady, and the blow had sent her spinning and falling. As she had fallen, she had crashed her head against the sewing-machine. Winifred claimed she had never intended to kill the old lady.

When she'd died, Winifred had panicked. At three o'clock in the morning following that assault, she had struggled to lift the body into a pram, no doubt using her nursing skills to cope with the cumbersome corpse, and in the darkness had wheeled it to the old pit shaft. She had managed to raise the cover to dump her great-aunt into the dark depths, then she had closed the cover and returned home. Later, when neighbours asked after Aunt

Emma, she had told them she had gone away, and then Winifred had had the audacity to forge Aunt Emma's signature to effect the sale of her house. That forgery earned her £300.

Winifred Hallaghan's husband never featured in the trial, but she was charged with murder. The magistrates at the committal proceedings considered the available evidence and reduced the charge to one of manslaughter. Winifred was also charged with three counts of forgery. When she appeared at Leeds Assizes in March 1949, she pleaded guilty to all charges. She was sentenced to five years' imprisonment, concurrent on all accounts.

8   Murders from the Fells and Dales

There is little doubt that many unexplained deaths have
occurred on the wild and lofty fells of the Yorkshire Dales.
In bygone days, when life was cheap, people were done to
death for a variety of reasons, ranging from jealousy in
love to robbery of their cash, and many carcases were left
to rot on the open moors. Many victims were itinerant
traders, some were wanderers, others were drovers, and
many lived a roaming life, so that a long absence from
their usual haunts or home was not unusual. If they died,
no one missed them, and so no search was organized;
their bodies might lie undiscovered for years while their
killers were never brought to justice.

Some deaths were from natural causes – lonely
travellers got lost and froze to death, others died from
disease or injury, and so an accurate toll of death upon
those open moors will never be known. From time to time
people vanished from their village homes, never to be
seen again, and there was always speculation that such
absent neighbours had either been murdered or fallen
down a mine or died a lonely death on the inhospitable
fells.

Even in recorded cases, our information is very slight, in
some cases coming only from the occasional newspaper
cutting which is reinforced by folk-memory or locally
written poems. The formal records of the time have long
since been destroyed.

Many met their end through unfortunate accidents. At

Silkstone, near Barnsley for example, the churchyard contains a stone monument bearing the names of twenty-six children. They were victims of a sudden flood during the summer of 1838 – they were working down the mines at the time. Seven of the boys were under ten years old, and one of the girls was only eight years of age. Another village that has suffered from flood is Holmfirth, now famous as the setting for the BBC TV series *Last of the Summer Wine*. In 1852 the Bilberry Reservoir above the village burst its dam, and some 90 million gallons of water poured down the dale. The village contains reminders of that awful flood, with pillars indicating its depth as it swirled through the village. Almost a hundred people lost their lives as houses, bridges and other buildings were swept away.

A tour of the Dales can reveal other interesting monuments, such as one at Wragby, near Wakefield, which records the death of Sarah Mellard in 1842 – she served as a maid at Nostell Priory for an amazing eighty-three years. At Manfield on the Yorkshire side of Teesdale, the churchyard contains the grave of a lady who was still working on a farm at the age of 108. An obelisk in the churchyard at Bolton-on-Swale records the death of a local man called Henry Jenkins who died on 6 December 1670 at the amazing age of 169, one of England's oldest inhabitants. But did Henry really live to be 169? At the age of 162, he said he could remember Henry VIII and the Battle of Flodden Field 152 years earlier. He said that Henry VIII was in France during the battle, that the earl of Surrey was general, and that he, Henry Jenkins, was ten or twelve at the time and recalled having gone to Northallerton with a cartload of arrows. When a historian checked these statements, she learned that the earl of Surrey had been a general at the Battle of Flodden Field, that bows and arrows were still being used at that time and that Henry VIII had been in Tournay. There are still arguments about the truth of the great age of Henry

Jenkins who, if his claims were correct, lived through nine reigns and experienced such national events as the Reformation, the Great Plague and the Great Fire of London.

Another mystery occurred at Hooton Roberts in the Don Valley, where three skeletons were found buried near the altar of the parish church, one of them being headless. They were discovered in 1895 during alterations to the building and were later thought to be those of the first earl of Strafford, his wife and daughter. The mystery here is that a monument to the earl had been erected some distance away, at Wentworth Woodhouse, and everyone thought that was his burial place – his widow lived near Hooton Roberts church after his death, and she was known to have been buried in the chancel in 1688. Thomas Wentworth, the first earl of Strafford, was beheaded on Tower Hill in London in 1641, so was this skeleton his mortal remains or not?

Another curious memorial to a noble family is at Barnburgh, near Doncaster; this is a memorial to the Cresacre family, one of whom was killed by a wild cat. He was Sir Percival Cresacre who died in 1477 after fighting the cat in the porch of the church; a wild cat later featured in the family's coat of arms.

Although memorials to murder victims of the past are not so prominent, one case came to my notice through a long poem. The location was a tiny hamlet which was once the most northerly community in Yorkshire. It used to lie within the North Riding of Yorkshire. Today, due to the boundary changes of 1974, it lies within County Durham but, as a matter of history, it can be included in this volume of stories from the Yorkshire Dales.

The hamlet is Holwick, which stands on what used to be the Yorkshire side of the River Tees under the shadow of Cronkley Fell. What remains of Holwick overlooks the Tees between the village of Middleton-in-Teesdale and the magnificent High Force, which is England's largest waterfall with a drop of over seventy feet. Today the only reminders of that old village are some scattered farms and a pub called the Strathmore Arms. In 1794 this remote community was the scene of a shocking murder.

An elderly shepherd called William Robinson lived in a ramshackle hut near Hungry Hill Farm not far from the inn. His only companion was his faithful dog. William was about sixty years old and looked after himself. He made a rough living by feeding off the products of his own patch of land and keeping a cow and some sheep. He appeared to be very contented with his simple life and rarely left the area. It was said that the grandest place he had ever seen was Barnard Castle, about ten miles away. He was a poor man who had never harmed anyone and, to the knowledge of those who knew him, he had no enemies. But on a chill day in April that year he was found dead on Holwick Fell.

He had been savagely killed and his throat was cut. His sheepdog sat near him, occasionally licking his face and trying to revive his beloved master. It was thought that the motive for this brutal crime was robbery, for it was rumoured that William Robinson had some money tucked away in his old shack, but no one can be quite sure.

His murderer was never caught. The whole sad story is recorded in rhyme. One verse says:

The ravens croak'd o'er yonder town
'Tis said that they could tell,
Who took the knife and slew the man
Found dead on Holwick Fell.

A similar tale is told of a murder higher up the dale; in this case an elderly recluse called Phyllis Bell was murdered in her shack, which was known as Snout House. It was near Cauldron Snout, a gorge through which the infant Tees roars and tumbles down a huge staircase of rock which is over 200 feet in length. Since the time of this killing, Cow Green Reservoir has been constructed, and it has facilities for nature study and angling, but the area around it is bleak and forbidding.

It was said that Phyllis was murdered for the hoard of gold she was supposed to have accumulated, but in fact she had no money. Her ghost, cloaked in red, is still said to haunt the scene of her death. In 1878 a skeleton was found in a cave known as Fairy Hole in Upper Teesdale, and some thought it might be the remains of Phyllis Bell. It had been buried in eight or nine feet of soil, and subsequent examination showed it to be that of a woman, but one from the cave-dwelling era.

Deeper into the Yorkshire Dales, the discovery of a woman's skeleton buried in peat added a neat factual emphasis to a legend which had for years circulated in Coverdale. This is a very remote valley and perhaps one of Yorkshire's most secluded; it extends south-west from Middleham in Wensleydale. A local legend was that the ghost of a woman in black, always shaking her head as if in a torment of some kind, walked the moors near Courting Wall Corner. So realistic was this apparition that some travellers once asked her to open a gate – but she then vanished. The story behind this haunting was that the woman had had two lovers, eventually rejecting one in favour of the other. The rejected man was consumed with jealousy and took her high onto Middleham Moor, where he killed her and buried her in the peat. She returned to haunt the area for years afterwards. The later discovery of that female skeleton, plus a piece of black cloth found buried nearby, did add strength to that ancient tale.

Another legend which has a sound factual base concerns the aptly named Deadman's Hill. This was originally known as Nidderhow and lies beneath Little Whernside; it was upon the route of a drovers' road which ran from Coverdale into Nidderdale via the now abandoned hamlet of Lodge. Today Deadman's Hill is shown on the maps and is located between the village of Horsehouse and Scar House Reservoir. The area still known as Lodge is near the northern banks of that reservoir.

According to local folk-memory, Deadman's Hill was the scene of a savage murder when three Scottish drovers or packmen (pedlars) were beheaded and buried in the peat bogs near the hamlet of Lodge. With the discovery of the three headless bodies in 1728, rumours abounded, one of them being that they were slaughtered by a woman and her daughters who kept an inn upon the drovers' route. One old account claims that the three women were arrested and admitted having drugged the Scotsmen's beer before killing them to obtain their ponies, plaids and cash.

It seems that the rumours did have some foundation, although there appears to be no account of anyone being found guilty of this crime. Indeed, the records suggest that no one was ever charged with it. Even so, rumours do persist, and one story says that the three women were found guilty and that they were hanged at Deadman's Hill. But this seems to be mere storytelling.

Nonetheless, the facts do appear to indicate that three Scotsmen were lured into a house so that they could be robbed and then killed. The men were regular visitors to this area, travelling twice a year from Scotland with their herds of cattle, and when they failed to return home, their relatives decided to arrange a search. Their enquiries traced them as far as this point; indeed, they were traced to the very house in which they had died, but there was insufficient evidence to level a charge against anyone, let alone secure a conviction.

It seems that upon their death, their corpses were conveyed by sledge across the moors and were buried precisely upon the boundary between two parishes. That boundary also formed the boundary between the North Riding and West Riding of Yorkshire, and it seems that this odd choice of burial place was made in the hope that it would confuse the authorities and so frustrate the progress of any justice. Today those county boundaries have vanished, for the area is now entirely within the county of North Yorkshire, although Deadman's Hill now sits upon other boundaries – that of the Yorkshire Dales National Park and a local authority district boundary which passes through here.

There is some documentary evidence to support the claim that this was a factual murder and not merely a legend. It seems that the killing was deliberate, because the heads were severed to prevent identification of the corpses if found, and there is no record of those heads being recovered.

In an old Middlesmoor township book dated 30 May 1728, there is confirmation that three bodies were buried at Lodge Edge without their heads. This was the formal funeral of the remains. The entry shows the following:

Expenses at the time to the coroner – 13s. 4d.
For sending warrants into Coverdale – 8d.
For carrying the biers – 6d.
To the sexton for making the graves – 1s. 6d.
To Anthony Handley for conveying the
    murdered bodies away when found – 1s. 0d.

A rather similar murder occurred during the early years of the last century in Wensleydale when a Scottish laird decided to visit Askrigg Fair. He made the mistake of daring to travel alone – a mistake because it was known that people travelling to fairs often had money upon them. A local farmer and his son discovered the laird upon his long route and decided to get their hands on his cash. They led him along a quiet lane under the pretext of guiding him along the correct route, but they killed him. Their callous crime was witnessed, however. A young man and his girlfriend were walking along the lane and saw everything that happened, but they were corrupt too

– the farmer paid them a share of the wealth, and so they all buried the poor visitor in a peat grave. Later the body was found by a peat-cutter who recognized it from the plaid he wore.

The unfortunate Scotsman was later given a proper burial in the churchyard at Grinton, near Reeth in Swaledale. For years afterwards, few people dared to travel alone to Askrigg Fair, for it earned a widespread and evil reputation through this killing.

Among the more notorious of Yorkshire murderers is a member of the aristocracy. He was Sir Walter Calverley, and his crime has created a curious mystery involving William Shakespeare.

The crime was committed in Shakespeare's time, probably in 1605, and it brought everlasting shame on this noble family. The Calverleys had lived in the village of Calverley for more than 600 years, tracing their ancestry to the time of William the Conqueror. Their stately mansion was eventually turned into flats for workmen, and the estate chapel became a wheelwright's shop.

The family was eminent in British life, their surname being Scott before they assumed the name of de Calverley in the fourteenth century. One of them married the daughter of Malcolm Canmore, King of Scotland. Another, also called Walter, became a friend of Joseph Addison, the poet, hymn-writer, essayist and author whose career also included politics. Addison became a Lord Commissioner for Trade in 1716 and Secretary of State in 1717. He wrote for many periodicals and newspapers, including *The Spectator*, in which one of his characters was Sir Roger de Coverley. This creation represented country gentlemen in Addison's highly popular column and it is said that Sir Roger was modelled upon Sir Walter Calverley. Even their names are similar – Calverley and Coverley.

But it was another Sir Walter who brought disgrace upon the family name. Young and rather wild, Walter went to Cambridge University. It is claimed that he consorted with Guy Fawkes and was involved with other gunpowder conspirators at Scotton, near Knaresborough in Nidderdale.

It was while he was at Cambridge that he fell in love with a girl far below his station in life. She was a humble village lass, not at all suitable for his future role as head of the Calverley family. At the time young Calverley was the ward of Lord Cobham, and it was thought desirable that he should marry Cobham's granddaughter. She was far more suitable; she had the right breeding and the right connections, and so the marriage was forced upon young Walter. Thus he married Philippa, daughter of the Hon. Henry Brooke, who was the fifth son of the fourth Baron Cobham. For a while the couple were happy and looked forward to the time when their family would inherit the estate, but children were a long time arriving. Eventually Walter grew to hate his wife, but then she did give birth to three fine sons. Even though he now had a family, he could not tolerate the woman he had been forced to marry, and it seems this caused him to stray from the ideal path of a gentleman of his class.

Apparently he also became obsessed with the belief that he was barren and that he could not therefore be the true father of his sons. He pointed out that it had taken many years for his sons to arrive and remarked on the friendship between his wife and his own best friend, a man called Leventhorpe. He began to suggest that Leventhorpe had fathered the children. In spite of repeated assurances by his wife, he insisted on this belief and began to drink. He got heavily into debt and went as far as mortgaging his estate in order to pay off his creditors. He entertained lavishly and, by contrast, became subjected to terrible bouts of depression. On one occasion he allowed his younger brother to be arrested instead of himself, and his enormous problems caused him to break down under the strain.

One fateful night, after drinking heavily, his hatred overwhelmed him and he galloped home full of fury. It seems he had lost all his control, because he entered his fine house, dispatched the servants on all kinds of fictitious errands to get them out of the way and then selected a particularly sharp dagger. He found his eldest son playing in the hall and stabbed him three or four times; next he found his second son and stabbed him in the heart. His wife came to see what was happening and rushed forward to save her children, but she was stabbed in the stomach. The third son was away from home in the care of a foster-mother and, Calverley having carried out this awful crime, then rode off to destroy that remaining child.

By now, the alarm had been raised and a hue-and-cry was raised in an attempt to halt this madman. He had a strong lead, but providence was on the side of that child – Walter's horse stumbled and fell. He was thrown off and, although he did mount to resume his evil journey, he was caught by his own servants before he could do any more harm.

Under arrest, he was first taken to the local magistrate at Kippax near Leeds, Sir John Bland. Calverley told him he had planned his attack for four years in the belief that none of the children was his own.

He was committed for trial at York Castle where, in 1605, he was charged with murdering his two sons. But he refused to plead, and this meant he would have to submit to '*peine forte et dure*' – being pressed with heavy weights until he made a plea. Without a plea, the trial could not proceed. But Calverley refused, and as more weights were added, he died under the pressure. Thus he never faced a trial for his crimes and so he was never found guilty. This might have been his last act of bravery; it might have been done to expiate his crime – because had he been found guilty of murder, his estate would have been forfeited to the Crown. Thus Calverley died without subjecting his heirs to that disgrace or the inevitable social and financial ruin.

Philippa, having been stabbed in the stomach, survived the attack and later remarried, her new husband being Sir Thomas Burton. Her youngest son lived to inherit the estate.

Many of the Calverleys lie buried within the churchyard at Calverley, which is between Shipley and Leeds, some four miles from Bradford, but it is not a church memorial that has left us with the broad outline of this story.

In 1608, some three years after Calverley's execution and eight years before Shakespeare's death, a play appeared which was based on these murders. It was called *A Yorkshire Tragedy* and subtitled *Two Most Unnatural and Bloodie Murthers by Master Calverley, a Yorkshire gentleman, upon his wife and two children, 1605*. It bore the note, 'A Yorkshire Tragedy, not so new as lamentable; written by Mr Shakespeare; acted by his Majesties Players at the Globe, 1608. London 1619. With a portrait of the brat at nurse.'

Along with some twenty other plays of doubtful authorship, this was once listed as having been written by Shakespeare, but scholars no longer accept that this is his work. But no one knows the identity of the real author.

One of the saddest of stories about crimes in the Yorkshire Dales relates to the victim of a cruel murder in 1759. She has become known as 'Mary of Romanby', her real name being Mary Ward, and her unfortunate death became the subject of a lengthy ballad entitled 'A Ballad on the Romanby Tragedy'. Through this poem, with its forty-two verses, Mary's death has become part of Yorkshire folklore, although the original crime was genuine.

Mary Ward lived in a small cottage in the village of Morton-on-Swale, which lies about four miles from Northallerton upon the A684 road which leads into Wensleydale.

Northallerton is one of North Yorkshire's market towns and, although far smaller than, say, York, Harrogate or Scarborough, it is the county town for North Yorkshire, which is England's largest county. Morton-on-Swale is a tiny community which lies midway between Northallerton and the crossing of the A1 trunk road at Leeming Bar. As its name suggests, it lies close to the River Swale as it emerges from Swaledale to meander through the broad Vale of Mowbray. This huge, flat valley covers about 400 square miles of countryside between North Yorkshire's two national parks, the Yorkshire Dales National Park and the North York Moors National Park, and through it run England's primary north–south routes, the A1 trunk road (the Great North Road) and the London–Edinburgh railway line.

Morton-on-Swale is a quiet community which now serves as a dormitory village for Northallerton. Its one claim to any kind of fame is that it was the place where Mary of Romanby was murdered. Romanby, where Mary worked, lies on the outskirts of Northallerton and now forms part of the town. Indeed, North Yorkshire's county hall and Northallerton railway station both lie within the old parish of Romanby, although they bear Northallerton addresses.

Although Romanby's identity has largely been lost, the older centre of the village can still be seen, with its attractive village green and tiny packhorse bridge. Romanby lies about two miles from Morton-on-Swale, and it was at Romanby that Mary Ward obtained work.

We do not know the name of her employer, although he was a gentleman of wealth who commanded respect in the neighbourhood. He lived at Reformation Manor Hall, which had oak-lined walls, latticed windows concealed by roses and briars, and a huge entrance hall displaying shields of warrior knights, suits of armour and helmets. There was an old baronial room with paintings, a carved mantelpiece, rich furnishings and good-quality furniture.

The house also had vaults and secret rooms.

It seems that Mary was as happy as a girl of her class might be, for her work was secure and the manor was beautiful, but this blissful home concealed a sombre secret. Unknown to anyone, the master of the house and his friends were crooks; they were coiners, men who faked the coinage of the realm. One of their skills was to file down gold and silver coins and collect the precious metal dust and filings which they then melted down and fashioned into realistic counterfeits. This was a felony, a most serious crime which ranked with murder and treason, and it carried the death penalty. But the wealth that coining could generate was often considered worth the risks. The work could be done in secret and required only a small space in which to operate.

The rooms concealed within that house at Romanby were ideal. Other than the perpetrators, no one knew of their presence. Then, quite by accident, Mary discovered the secret. A door had been left open as the master had been called away on some urgent business, and this quiet servant girl found herself staring at the apparatus of master coiners. She knew what this meant. She knew that her master was a criminal; suddenly all the events of the past months held a new significance, and she realized she was working within a den of rogues. But she did not leave. She continued with her job, but she could not resist telling a boyfriend of her discovery.

As gossiping youngsters love to do, she told him all about the secret room and its contents, but unknown to Mary, her friend was a member of the coining gang. He told his leader of Mary's discovery. That sealed her fate. She could not be relied upon to keep this vital secret, because she talked far too much. The coiners therefore held a meeting and decided that, if Mary was allowed to live, she would surely talk again, and next time their secret might reach the ears of the authorities. Mary could not be sacked, for that would encourage her to tell tales out of spite, and so this group of men decided she must die.

In an attempt to conceal their guilt and to maintain their guise as men of quality, they produced a most elaborate plot, with Mary as the central figure.

One Sunday night in summer, as the moon highlighted the beautiful gardens of the house at Romanby, a messenger on horseback arrived at the door. His loud shouting and knocking managed to arouse Mary from her slumbers, and when she asked his business, he said his mission was urgent. She did not know the man, but he told her that he had been sent by her mother, who was dying. The man said that Mrs Ward did not have long to live and that she had requested Mary's presence at her bedside during her final hours. Clearly this upset Mary, but she said she could not leave the house without the consent of her master, so the rider said he would wait while she sought his permission; Mary could then join him on his horse, and they would ride two-up to Mrs Ward's home at Morton-on-Swale.

Mary hurried upstairs to her master's bedroom and tried to rouse him to make her urgent request, but she could not waken him. Try as she might, the man would not open his eyes, and Mary was becoming more and more anxious as the minutes ticked away. It now seems that the master was feigning sleep at this time; that way, he could deny any knowledge of the affair. Mary, however, now had a difficult decision to make. She realized she could not abandon her dying mother in her desperate time of need, and so she crept up to her room to dress for the journey. Meanwhile the horseman waited outside.

In the candlelight, Mary noticed that her Bible lay open at a peculiar passage from the Book of Job – it said, 'They shall seek me in the morning and shall not find me; and where I am, they shall not come.'

Perhaps this prophecy did cause her to hesitate, but the desire to be at her mother's side overcame all her fears and, after locking the doors of the house, she crept out of a casement window to ride away with the messenger. He stressed the urgency of the moment by saying they must ride swiftly, otherwise the life of Mary's mother would be gone. Ahead lay a journey of around three miles, for Mrs Ward lived in a cottage close to Morton Bridge; a bridge still crosses the River Swale at this point, although it may not be the one that Mary knew. The rider spurred his horse into a fast gallop, and so Mary was carried into the night. The hour was late because, as the old ballad says, 'The ale house was mute within.' The verses tell us that it was a night of nature's calm, with the earth and sky very still and the stream's flow so tranquil as the summer moon sweetly shone.

The entire journey would take less than an hour, but before reaching Morton Bridge, the rider halted his horse and told Mary she was to die. He reminded her of the secrets she had uncovered, and warned her of the dangers of being too free with her tongue. His words were cruel and determined. She pleaded with him, asking to see her mother before she was killed, but the man refused. He said her babbling tongue would make a morsel for the worms and she must die immediately.

Mary leapt off the horse and ran for her life. She managed to cross a field before reaching a wood; she knew the wood, for she had played here as a child. She knew every path, every glade and every hiding-place, and if only she could gain the security of those dark trees, she would evade him and be safe.

But now there were three men in pursuit. The other two had been lying in wait at this point, the halting-place having been pre-planned, and all gave chase as the fleet-footed Mary approached the wood. There was a stile which led into the trees – she knew it well; but in the darkness, even if it was lit by the moon, Mary had missed the stile. She had run to the wrong place and, as the men closed upon her, she tried to scramble over the thorny hawthorn hedge, hauling herself over by grasping the bough of an overhanging tree. But the branch broke and threw Mary into the hedge; the noise created by the breaking branch and her struggle to free herself from the thorns alerted the men, and they caught her. Mary fought for her life; one account says the men broke both her arms in that desperate struggle, but Mary died a gallant death.

It was said that her battered body was buried on a piece of waste ground near Morton Bridge, but it was never found. Later, when the story of her cruel death began to circulate, a search was made for Mary's remains, but they were never traced. For this reason, no prosecution for murder was ever mounted, although some accounts suggest that one man was brought to justice.

This is doubtful, for no trace of Mary has ever been found, and so there would be no real evidence of their crime. It was claimed that all the villagers knew of her fate, which is how the story has survived to this day, and for years afterwards the broken branch of the tree which collapsed under Mary's desperate leap for freedom was shown to visitors.

Even today it is said that the ghost of Mary of Romanby haunts the banks of the River Swale at Morton Bridge. She makes her appearance on the anniversary of her death, as the church clock at nearby Ainderby Steeple strikes midnight.

Reformation Manor Hall, in which the secret coining room was discovered by Mary, was later demolished and no trace remains; it stood on the edge of the village green at Romanby, almost opposite the site of the village well.

If the words of the ballad are all true, modern searchers might still find that grave if they dare, because Mary's ghost will reveal it. The verse says of Morton Bridge at night:

For Mary's spirit wanders there,
In snowy robe array'd,
To tell each trembling villager,
Where sleeps the murder'd maid.

9 From Hell, Hull and Halifax …

Although the phrase 'From Hell, Hull and Halifax, Good Lord Deliver Us' is still widely used, its origin may not be so well known. The saying was created by the ruffians and rogues of Yorkshire and was in use several centuries ago, being quoted by the so-called 'water poet', John Taylor (1580–1653).

This warning to wrong-doers came about because of the severe penalties administered to convicts in Hull and Halifax.

By the sixteenth century, Hull's gallows and gibbets were positioned at low-water mark so that they were within the jurisdiction of the Admiralty. This was because in 1451 the mayor of Hull, who owned the gallows, was also chief officer of the Admiralty in his capacity of Admiral of the Humber. Thus Hull's gallows dispensed justice for crimes which were committed on land or at sea. They consequently filled a gap in the prevailing legal system and there is little doubt that their efficiency led to fear across most of Yorkshire and probably further afield.

Halifax, on the other hand, had a more fearsome machine. The Halifax gibbett (spelt with two ts) was not a gibbet of the ordinary kind which displayed the executed bodies of criminals as a warning to others, but a machine which severed the heads of convicts. It was very similar to the French guillotine, named after its inventor, Joseph-Ignace Guillotine, which it preceded by many years, and it was in use long before the Scots produced a similar machine.

The Scottish one was devised by the Regent of Scotland, the Earl of Morton, who was invited to witness an execution at Halifax in 1565. After seeing the efficiency of the Halifax machine, he made a small working model and then returned to Scotland full of enthusiasm and determined to build a similar structure. Upon completion, it was nicknamed 'The Maiden'. That name might have come from the Celtic *mod-dun*, meaning a place where justice was administered. Tradition says that Morton himself was the machine's first and last victim, but this is not so. Nonetheless, he did die upon his own invention, having been convicted of treason, but not until 2 June 1581, sixteen years after he built it.

Although the Halifax gibbett was much older than the Maiden, its precise origins are rather vague. Some accounts suggest that a similar device was in operation at the place now known as Halifax more than a thousand years ago. Overseas, the first guillotine-type of machine might have been used to behead Conrad of Swabia at Naples in 1266. In 1300 one was used to behead five men at Zittau in Germany. The Zittau device was created because the axemen who were usually employed for this grisly task were somewhat unreliable and clumsy and seemed incapable of making a clean severance, so a machine was devised for humanitarian reasons. In 1307 a similar machine was deployed in Ireland to execute Murcod Ballagh, near Merton.

It is known that the Halifax gibbett was in use during the reign of Edward III (1327–77), and as long ago as 1600 its invention was attributed to a monk. It is said that the king had granted to Halifax the right to execute criminals by hanging, but whenever an execution was imminent, no volunteer hangman could be found. Another method of execution had to be adopted and so a local friar developed 'a gin to chop off men's heads of itself'. There is no doubt that it proved highly efficient and successful, for it was in action on market days, usually Tuesdays, Thursdays and Saturdays.

Justice was swift: convicts were executed on the first market day following their conviction, and it was this swiftness that made the machine so terrifying to its potential victims. There was never more than a week between conviction and execution. While awaiting their execution, the convicts were placed in the stocks, with any stolen goods on display before them. They had to carry the stolen goods to the stocks and then to the site of the gibbett, the reason for putting them on display being that: 'Passengers might see them. And this was done in Terror to others that they might take warning by his wicked deeds, never to commit the like.'

Anyone caught stealing cloth or falsifying the coinage of the realm was rapidly sent here, as well as murderers, rapists, robbers, horse-thieves and sundry other convicts. The penalty of execution for stealing cloth was especially created for the area around Halifax during the seventeenth century. It was promulgated to protect its cloth industry. The district lay within the Forest of Hardwick, which constituted a Liberty in its own right and included eighteen towns and villages. All were involved with the manufacture of cloth, and when thieves began to prey upon the clothmakers before escaping into the more remote area of the forest, a law was drafted specifically to protect the cloth merchants and the livelihoods of the manufacturers.

A court was established at Halifax to try offenders, and the jury comprised the bailiff of Halifax, four jurymen from the town and four from the other townships. The local law said, 'If a felon be taken within the Liberty of the Forest of Hardwick, with goods stolen out or within the said precincts, either hand-habend, back-berand or confessioned, to the value of thirteen pence halfpenny, he shall after three market days or meeting days, within the town of Halifax, next after such his apprehension and being condemned, be taken to the gibbett and there have his head cut from his body.'

The gibbett was perfect for teaching such thieves a hard lesson. The gibbett was mounted on a huge square base faced with stone and with steps rising to it at one end. The twin uprights of the gibbett were at the other end of the block and stood fifteen feet high; a cross beam, four feet long, separated them at the top and held them steady.

Deep grooves in each of the uprights allowed the blade to rise and fall between the uprights. The blade was attached to a movable and weighted block; the blade was eighteen inches long by twelve inches wide. The victim lay beneath the blade and it was then drawn to its full height by a rope attached to the horse. When the horse had drawn the blade as high as possible by means of a rope and pulley, it was secured in that position by a peg. When that peg was withdrawn, the blade dropped to sever the victim's head. The peg was withdrawn when the bailiff or one of the jurors gave the signal to carry out the execution; when he raised a finger, the peg was pulled out and down came the heavy, sharp blade to achieve its awful purpose.

From time to time, a callous twist was introduced to an execution. If the thief had stolen a pig, a sheep, a goat, a horse or other animal, the animal in question was attached to the rope and given the privilege of hauling up the blade which would end the life of its taker. If no animal was involved, it was usual for a horse to draw up the blade, although sometimes teams of volunteers were called in, the reason being that no individual could then be held responsible for the death of the victim.

Records of all deaths on the Halifax gibbett are scant, but between 1541 and 1650 parish registers show that forty-nine people lost their heads beneath its blade. Twenty-five of them died during the reign of Elizabeth I (1558–1603), six of whom were women. In one case a father and daughter were executed within minutes of each other; in another case an unknown man, executed in 1542, never revealed his name, and his death was recorded as that of 'a certain stranger'.

The Halifax gibbett was last used in April 1650, when two men called John Wilkinson and Anthony Mitchell were executed for stealing nine yards of cloth worth 9 shillings and two young horses worth 48 shillings and 60 shillings respectively.

When the gibbett fell into disuse, its base and uprights were forgotten and lost. Then in 1840, when workmen were clearing space to lay out the People's Park, the base was discovered under a mound of earth. It was cleared to reveal the stonework in its original form. It stood some thirteen feet square by four feet high. The steps up which the victim had to climb to his death also remained.

After 1650 the blade of this machine was kept in storage at Wakefield, and it remained there for more than 300 years. Then, in 1970, it was returned to Halifax for display in the town's Bankfield Museum, alongside a model of the gibbett. The other remains of the infamous Halifax gibbett are also preserved and lie near the appropriately named Gibbett Street in Halifax, a reminder of a unique if harrowing period of judicial history. Halifax is thus the only place in England where executions were carried out by this method.

Since its earliest days, Halifax has been noted for the manufacture of woollens and textiles, its formal role beginning around 1414. Throughout its history, as with any other large and busy town, there have been many murders and mysteries, but it is a particularly curious killing that is said to have given Halifax its name. In its early days it was known as Horton but, according to this tale, the bizarre behaviour of a young monk earned it the name Halifax.

The story dates to the seventh century, when Whitby Abbey, on the Yorkshire coast, was under the stewardship of the powerful and intelligent Abbess Hilda. It was then known as Streonshalh, and England's first poet, Caedmon, was a cowman there. At that time one of the monks was called Aelred. He was a young man of around thirty or thirty-five, with a pale complexion and a rather emaciated frame. As a child he had been noted for his intelligence and dedication to learning, and it was no surprise that he became a monk.

He was very shy in the company of girls, however, and the more cruel of his contemporaries suggested he was terrified of them, especially the young, beautiful and blonde ones. Some said it was this fear of girls that was the real reason he had become a monk. There is no doubt he was a serious-minded character who had a great yearning for religion. In an attempt to deepen his faith, he spent a lot of his time fasting or undertaking long vigils and penances. He prayed a lot too, seeking help and guidance in his own battle to save his soul.

But he grew to feel that life enclosed in an abbey was too comfortable, and he decided to become a hermit in order to subject himself to even greater hardship in his pursuit of perfection and total holiness. He left Whitby and travelled into the wilds of Yorkshire, eventually finding a beautiful valley surrounded by hills and rich with tree-lined slopes. There was a dry cave too, and so Aelred settled here. It was in the fells above a village called Horton. He decided to make a door for the cave and furnished his new home with crudely made chairs, a table and a bed. Here he spent his time in prayer, breaking his routine only by travelling into the villages to preach the faith to those less fortunate than he. In addition to saving his own soul, he wished to save the souls of all the people around him and steeled himself to face them – especially any women who might become his followers.

There is little doubt that Aelred was happiest when alone; the spartan life in the woods appeared to suit him.

In time, he managed to construct a little chapel in this dale, and so the people now came to visit him. He was known for his love of God and his absolute faith; he said Mass and heard the confessions of his growing flock, he tended the sick and the lame, and it was very evident to the people that Aelred was indeed a truly holy man.

One lady who recognized his holiness asked him to help with her newly founded home for girls. Although this was not a convent, it relied on religious methods; the girls could leave to get married, for example, and they could grow their hair or wear nice clothes, but they lived a good, holy life while enclosed within its walls. The foundress asked Aelred if he would attend the home from time to time to say Mass, to hear the girls' confessions and to administer Holy Communion.

Father Aelred readily agreed, seeing this as a new opportunity to save souls, and he undertook his duties with all the solemnity of his calling. Then a new girl arrived. Aelred noticed her when he went to conduct the service of Benediction at the home. She was young and beautiful, with long, fair hair and blue eyes set in a charming face of the most exquisite complexion. Aelred could not take his eyes off her. He was spell-bound and began to experience feelings of the kind of which no holy priest should be aware. This disturbed him. He could not understand the effect she had upon him. He hurried back to his cell to pray for guidance, but each time he went to the home to say take services or hear confession, she was there.

Soon she was looking into his eyes and smiling at him. And those feelings within his breast and body became stronger and more powerful. For the holy Aelred, they were very worrying feelings. His fear of pretty blonde girls had evaporated to be replaced by something totally different, something that he failed to understand.

At his cell in the woods, he fasted, he prayed, he denied himself sleep and created hurtful penances, all with the aim of removing the thoughts that this beautiful girl had aroused in him. But nothing worked. He could not help thinking of her every minute of the day and night and, in his isolated world, he did not realize he was falling deeply in love with her.

Eventually it was time for her to make her confession to him, and she confessed her love for a holy man – it was some time before Aelred realized she was talking about him. He could not believe his ears. He looked upon the beautiful girl, and when she looked into his eyes, he experienced everything that showed the truth of her words. She loved him, and he knew that he loved her. He found himself wanting this lovely creature ... but he was a priest ...

Tormented beyond belief, he hurried yet again to his cell, where he prayed for enlightenment, and that night, as his tormented body and desperately sick mind wrestled with his dilemma, the truth confronted him. His faith was strong, he knew, and his belief in God had told him the truth.

He realized that the lovely, fair-haired girl was not in love with him at all; he decided that she was not a fair maiden – she was the devil in disguise. Aelred knew that he must deal once and for all with the devil. It was Satan in the image of this delightful girl! He must rid himself of Satan ... and so he made his plans.

The next time she came to his cell to confess her sins and to declare her love once more, he was waiting with a knife. In a mad rage, he shouted, 'Satan, I know thee and I defy thee!' and he stabbed the poor girl in the heart. She fell to the ground of his cave, fatally wounded and bleeding. He then carried out an even more dreadful deed. He cut off her head as he screamed, 'Thy head shall be placed aloft as a warning to others.'

Aelred, now totally mad, carried the bleeding head into the woods near his cell and placed it in an ancient yew tree where the trunk split into several branches. The eerie head peered out at him. Then he ran higher into the wood, screaming in joy at his defeat of Satan's machinations.

When the young girl did not return to the home, the

other inmates began a search, knowing she had walked to the cave of the hermit to make her weekly confession. There they found her headless body but no sign of Father Aelred. They must find her head and they must find the priest, and so the hunt continued all that night and into the following day.

Next morning the body of Father Aelred was discovered at the foot of a high cliff. He was dead. It was not known whether he had fallen down in his excited state or whether he had killed himself in remorse following the awful murder of the young girl.

Later the head of the girl was found, still in its place among the branches of the yew tree. When an attempt was made to remove it, it was found that the hair had apparently grown to take root upon the bark of the tree, and so it was impossible to remove it from this place. This was considered a miracle by the simple people, and so the head was left in place, and thus the tree became a holy shrine. People came from far and wide to look upon the tree with its fixed virgin's head, and to take away pieces of its twigs or leaves in the belief they possessed holy or miraculous powers. The bark revealed tiny hair-like ridges which they believed to be the growing hair of the virgin.

The head was allowed to remain there for many years as a holy relic. Even in its skeletal state, it remained a reminder of an awful crime.

But following this dreadful murder the pilgrims renamed Horton. They called it 'Halig-Fax', which means 'Holy Hair'; that name is now Halifax.

Or so the story says!

Whether that tale is pure legend, or a mixture of legend and fact, is something we shall never know, but modern Halifax has produced its own mystery killing. The year was 1957 and the victim was an elderly lady called Emily Pye who ran a small grocery shop in Gibbett Street.

On the afternoon of Whit Saturday, 8 June 1957,

someone entered Emily's shop, viciously attacked her and left her dead on the floor of the living-quarters with severe head wounds. She was eighty years old. She had run her little corner-shop for more than thirty years, and it stocked virtually all the basic daily requirements for the neighbouring houses – tinned foods, soap, sweets, cigarettes and other essential products. It was not a large or wealthy premises, but it served the locality, and it had provided Emily with her livelihood for a large part of her life.

That afternoon Halifax was quiet. It was a public holiday, and many of the townspeople, including Emily's neighbours in Gibbett Street, had gone away for the day. Some had left to explore the dales, some to visit relations and some to seek sunshine along the Yorkshire coast. But Emily had remained in her shop, for there was always someone who wanted something ...

It being such a quiet day, Emily's niece decided she would invite her aunt to tea; she would suggest that Aunt Emily close her shop and join them at Northowram for the rest of that day. It would be a nice break for the old lady.

But when Emily's niece arrived at the shop at three o'clock, it was closed and the doors were locked and bolted. She and her husband knocked loudly and shouted her name, but there was no reply, and each realized that this was not normal. Aunt Emily never went anywhere, and she most certainly would not have locked the shop at this time of the day ... besides, why did she not respond to their knocking and shouting.

Worried, they called the police. A policeman arrived and made a brief survey, knocking and shouting as the couple had, and due to their concern he decided to break in. They gave their consent. The door was smashed open and the policeman entered the premises. He found the body of Emily Pye on the floor of her living-room, partially covered by a rug. She had severe head injuries and she was dead.

It did not require a forensic expert to realize that this was murder, and an inquiry was launched without delay. At that time, Halifax's police force was not part of the West Riding Constabulary. Halifax Borough Police was a small force with limited resources, and its officers lacked the expertise to investigate a potentially protracted or difficult murder case. The chief constable, Mr Gerald Goodman, wasted no time calling in a team of detectives from New Scotland Yard. At that time this was common practice; it was a service provided by the Metropolitan Police in London for smaller, provincial police forces which lacked the vital skills needed for such major investigations.

In those areas, 'difficult' murders occurred very infrequently. Many murders were easily solved, often being the outcome of domestic strife or local violence, but Mr Goodman realized this one was different. From the outset, it had the appearance of a difficult crime to solve – the absence of clues, the lack of witnesses, the open premises at which anyone might call and the fact that that day was a public holiday when anyone, coming from a wide area, might have popped into Emily's little shop without raising suspicions.

The Yard dispatched to Halifax Detective Superintendent Herbert Hannan and Detective Sergeant Christopher Rowe, and they began work immediately. Their first task was to find anyone who had been in Gibbett Street on that Saturday afternoon between noon and 3 p.m.

Only four people came forward, and one of them could assure the detectives that Emily had been alive at 12.20 p.m. It emerged that a violent thunderstorm had occurred during the afternoon, and it had driven everyone indoors. Had it driven the killer into the shop? Indeed, had it drowned the cries of poor Emily? But no one else could help with information about callers between 12.20 p.m. and 3 p.m. Thus, out of a population of almost 100,000 people, only four said they had been in the vicinity at the material time, and only one of those, the one who had seen Emily alive at 12.20 p.m., could add anything useful to the inquiry. The police had no reason to suspect a reluctance to come forward – it was simply that most of the residents were away.

The pathologist, Dr David Price, could add little either, although he did confirm that death had taken place between noon and 3 p.m. that Saturday afternoon, but he could not be more precise. He did add, however, that in his opinion Emily had first been assaulted with bare knuckles before dying of head wounds, and that the weapon which killed her had been one of the irons from her own fireside. Those irons revealed no useful evidence such as fingerprints or fibres.

A meticulous search of the premises, both the house and the shop, suggested that the murderer had spent a very limited time inside. A small amount of cash had been taken from the till; it would be a very small amount due to the lack of customers on that quiet day, although Emily had stored larger sums upstairs. These comprised takings from her previous days of trading which had not been banked, but the intruder had not found that and, according to the available evidence, had not even searched for it.

It seemed that Emily's killer had entered the shop while she was in her living-quarters and, finding the counter unattended, had taken the opportunity to steal money from her till. She had probably come through to disturb him, whereupon he had lashed out with his fists. This might have knocked the old lady unconscious, where-upon she was taken into the living-quarters; if she was about to revive, he might have panicked and ended her life with a frenzied attack with the poker.

If this did happen, it does suggest that the killer was known to her. A stranger might have been content to knock her senseless before running for his freedom with the small amount of money.

Another pointer towards a local person is the fact that,

after killing Emily, the intruder bolted the front door of the shop from the inside and left by the side door, dropping the latch behind him. An opportunist thief would not have stayed behind long enough to do that. There is little doubt that Emily's killer hoped his crime would remain undiscovered for a long time, but at 3 p.m. Emily's niece called to set in motion this difficult and unsuccessful investigation.

The police made exhaustive enquiries in Yorkshire and elsewhere, checking places where itinerants might be found, such as hostels and lodging-houses, and places from which loners might have been absent at the material time. Enquiries along the routes into and out of Halifax failed to produce any sightings of hitchhikers or others who might be attempting to gain lifts from cars and lorries. No bloodstained people had been sighted, nor was any such clothing discovered. Local enquiries produced no information and over the following weeks continued to yield nothing useful, and so by the Christmas of 1947 the inquiry was brought to an end. Nothing further could be done. The men from Scotland Yard went back to their offices in London, and the local police returned to normal duties in Halifax.

In spite of detailed and protracted enquiries, the killer of Emily Pye has never been traced, and the file remains open.

If her assailant had been detected at that time, he would have faced death by hanging, while so very close to Emily's old shop stands a reminder of Halifax's unique form of justice – the remains of the infamous Halifax gibbett. The fear of Hell, Hull or Halifax did not deter this criminal.

10   The Leeds Rippers

The man who first used the name of 'Ripper' for a particularly vicious form of attack upon women was the sadistic killer who has entered the annals of criminal history under the name of 'Jack the Ripper'. In 1888 a series of six murders occurred in the Whitechapel area of London. All the victims were women, and all suffered similar knife wounds, incisions and mutilations to the body which suggested that the killer was someone with anatomical knowledge, such as a surgeon, a doctor or even a butcher. In spite of widespread publicity and intense police investigations at the time, followed by repeated and new investigations during the years which have followed, the identity of the murderer remains utterly unknown.

From time to time strong circumstantial evidence is produced which tends to indicate the name of one or another of several likely suspects, but no positive identification has ever been made. Many names have been suggested, ranging from a member of the royal family to known members of the medical profession, but none has been proved to be Jack the Ripper. One of his trademarks was to taunt the police with letters about his crimes and, following much speculation and fear in London, he sent a note to the police which said:

I'm not a butcher,
Nor a yid,

Nor yet a foreign skipper,
But I'm your own light-hearted friend,
Yours truly, Jack the Ripper.

From that time, the murderer became known as 'Jack the Ripper', but unlike the nicknames of today's criminals, that name was coined by the killer himself and not by the press or the public. The name was also used in the rhyming slang of the district to indicate a kipper, and it was used by Australian tailors to indicate someone who was worthless and idle.

Almost a century after the crimes of Jack the Ripper there was another Ripper. From his first attack in July 1975 until his arrest in August 1980, the activities of a man who also attacked or killed several women in widespread parts of the north of England earned him the nickname 'the Yorkshire Ripper'. But unlike Jack the Ripper, the Yorkshire Ripper was eventually arrested and convicted. He was later identified as Peter Sutcliffe, who was charged with having murdered thirteen women and attempting to murder a further seven. Many of his crimes were in or around Leeds and other parts of West Yorkshire. He was sentenced to life imprisonment for his crimes. There is no value in chronicling his activities in a work of this nature, for they have already received widespread coverage in articles and books.

But Leeds is the location of two more Ripper-style crimes in which women were murdered and the killer has never been traced ...

Leeds has many historic claims and boasts many fine buildings in addition to its superb city centre. Its grammar school was founded in 1552, although the city dates at least to the fourteenth century, since when it has become a major industrial and financial centre which boasts more trades within its boundaries than any other town. The oldest rail track in the world was laid here in 1758, and later it was used by a steam-engine invented by Matthew Murray several years before George Stephenson's famous *Rocket*.

Another of Leeds' pioneering men was a citizen of the city, albeit a six-foot-five-inch-tall Frenchman called Augustin le Prince. A very clever inventor, in 1885 he projected some of the world's first moving pictures and thus became one of the originators of the cinema. Among his pictures were some of horse-drawn vehicles crossing Leeds Bridge and others taken at Roundhay in Leeds. At Roundhay, he photographed Mrs Joseph Whitley of Oakwood Grange, so making her probably the first Englishwoman to appear in a moving picture. She died in 1888.

For these dramatic pictures, he used multiple cameras, some with several lenses so that they could take a sequence of photographs. There is little doubt that he was a genius of his craft.

He was annoyed that he could not perfect his idea, due to a lack of modern technology, but it seems that the invention of celluloid film enabled him to improve his techniques. The prospects afforded him by this development were exciting.

There was a great deal of work to be done, and le Prince knew he was on the threshold of a very exciting period in the history of photography; the projection of moving images was something entirely new, and he decided he must visit America with his invention. He had previously worked in the United States and felt a return visit would be beneficial. He wanted to interest the Americans in the progress he had made, and he must have sensed the world-wide interest and benefits that would surely follow.

Before setting sail for America, however, he went to France on a short business trip and made use of the opportunity to visit his brother at Dijon. Upon his departure from Dijon, his brother went with him to the railway station and bade farewell as Augustin boarded a train bound for Paris. The date was 16 September 1890. Augustin le Prince was never seen again, dead or alive. He simply vanished.

Extensive enquiries were made at the time, but nothing was ever again seen or heard of him. He had no known enemies, he was not a disagreeable or unbalanced individual; it seems he was a thoroughly nice, clever gentleman who was of distinctive appearance due to his height, and he just disappeared. The mystery remains.

Among the more unusual historic associations with Leeds are the world's first set of automatic traffic lights which were tested on the city's streets, and a bricklayer who invented Portland cement. He was Joseph Aspdin, who lived from 1779 until 1855; his statue is in the town hall.

Some of the town's major streets, business and shopping centres were once regarded as places where no decent person should go, especially when alone. One such area was around the part now known as Wellington Street, not far from the Queen's Hotel. It is now a major thoroughfare with shops and business premises. At the beginning of this century, however, it was a slum district, the haunt of prostitutes and others who preyed upon those less fortunate than themselves, such as thieves, tricksters, pickpockets and robbers of all kinds. One notorious part of this district was known as Millers Square, and this was the home of a woman called Kate Summerfield.

Kate, aged forty, had once been married, but her husband had left her to live overseas and so she lived with a labourer called John Studholme. Their shabby home was in a one-room rented flat, and they moved in during the winter of 1910, some time shortly before Christmas. It seems that Studholme was considered by his neighbours to be a decent person who was respectable and pleasant. Kate was described as cheerful, but she had enormous problems. She was an alcoholic, and she earned money for her upkeep and her heavy drinking by being a prostitute. She was not a high-class prostitute, for her clients were the rough and dirty down-and-outs of her own low-class neighbourhood. It was a very high-risk business.

At the time, Studholme was out of work and was having difficulty finding employment. He had very little money, and there is no doubt that Kate earned some necessary cash through her prostitution. But her clients were not wealthy and her income was not enough to sustain them. They fell behind with their rent, and by the first days of January 1911 they were deep in a financial crisis. This made Kate drink even more heavily. Worse came when their landlord decided to evict them. Their plight was desperate, and Kate knew only one way to earn the necessary extra cash very swiftly. She went out to seek some more clients.

It seems she was successful, because she found someone who agreed to pay for her services on condition he could stay overnight. Kate agreed to this. It meant, however, that John Studholme would have to stay away from home that night as she went about 'the business' with her client. She went into the town to find John and make her request to him. Kate located him around 5 p.m. that evening, Thursday 5 January 1911, and put her proposal to him. He listened and then, in desperate need of cash, he consented. He said that Kate could have exclusive use of the room that night.

She and John parted shortly afterwards. He was never again to see her alive. She was seen by other people, however. Between 7 p.m. and 8 p.m. a shopkeeper remembered her rushing into his corner shop to buy some tea and sugar, but she was in too much of a rush to wait for her change. As she hurried out with her purchases, she called out to him that she would collect the small amount of change the next day, as she had a man waiting for her at home.

Another man reported having seen Kate around

midnight. He said she was then staggering along Wellington Street, not far from her home, and he was emphatic that she was drunk. She was accompanied by a man whom the witness did not recognize – he knew it was not John Studholme but could not suggest another name. It seems that Kate was on her way home after a night's drinking in the town centre and that she was about to finalize the evening's entertainment of her client.

John Studholme, in the meantime, had gone to the Adelphi lodging-house for the night. The following morning he went into the town to visit a café for some breakfast. He was seen and identified at these places. Around 10 a.m. that same day, Friday 6 January, the day following Kate's assignation with her client, John returned to their home in Miller's Square. He found the house locked and the window shutters closed. He thought she was still entertaining her customer and so he went away for a while.

To pass the time, he went to the Nelson Inn, and it seems he spent about two hours there, popping backwards and forwards to the house but always finding it locked and shuttered. He hammered on the door and rattled the shutters, but there was no response. By lunchtime he sensed that something was desperately wrong and so he returned once again, this time determined to break in if Kate did not respond. Upon his final attempt to rouse her, he gained no response and so decided he must break in. He did so and saw that Kate was still apparently asleep in bed.

But when he opened the shutters to give light to the room, he was horrified to find the bed saturated with blood. It was clear that Kate was dead, apparently having been beaten savagely to death. John Studholme ran out to fetch a policeman, and soon a full-scale murder investigation was launched.

At that time Leeds police force was not part of the West Riding of Yorkshire Constabulary but was a small city police force in its own right. The chief constable was Mr George Tarry, and he had about 500 officers under his command. He placed Detective Superintendent Handley in charge of the enquiries.

From initial observations in the dingy room, the police found that Kate was still dressed in an underslip and black stockings. Her body was positioned along the bed in the form of a cross, with each arm extended and each hand lashed to the bedhead with a twisted apron and some bootlaces. In addition, she had been stabbed viciously about her body. There was a total of seventeen stab wounds, and they were all over the body – around the ribs, breasts, back, head and neck, but in addition to these terrible injuries her skull was fractured too.

A search for the supposed murder weapon led to a brick which was discovered near the fireplace, and it was found to have her hair and blood adhering to it. This was preserved for evidence as the likely murder weapon. There was a half-bottle of whisky nearby, and a knife was found in the kitchen sink. It seemed she had died from a vicious attack.

From the story given to them by John Studholme, it was evident that Kate had entertained her client in the room, where she had given him a cup of sugared tea; they seemed then to have gone out into the town for drinks before returning shortly after midnight with a bottle of whisky. Some time after midnight and before 10 a.m. on Friday 6 January 1911, Kate Summerfield had been savagely murdered.

But the post-mortem examination showed that she had not died from the stab wounds, nor had she died from the fractured skull. Indeed, the knife found in the kitchen sink was not the one which had caused her wounds, although the brick had been used to strike her about the head. She had been suffocated. The post-mortem examination showed that the cause of her death was asphyxia and that the horrific injuries had been caused after death. It was also thought that her body had been tied in that odd crucifix shape after death because the bonds were not tight enough to have held her there had she struggled to escape.

As this was only some twenty-two or three years after the activities of Jack the Ripper in London, there were the inevitable comparisons, but the London killer was never a suspect for Kate's murder. The chief suspect was, of course, John Studholme. He was interviewed at length by the investigating officers and spent most of that Friday in the City Police Headquarters at Leeds under interrogation. But when his movements were checked, he was able to prove his whereabouts throughout the material times. It was clear to the police that John Studholme had not killed Kate Summerfield.

Apart from the man seen in Wellington Street with Kate on the night before her death, no other suspect was brought within the scope of the investigation. The killing was grotesque because of the mutilation of her body after being suffocated, but all enquiries failed to trace the killer of Kate Summerfield.

A similarly bizarre murder occurred in Scarcroft, a village on the outskirts of Leeds. At the turn of this century it was a small, unpretentious place comprising a few farms and cottages and the remnants of an old moat. It lay upon the route of a Roman road which ran from west to east and today lies just west of the A58 Wetherby–Leeds trunk road. Now it is unrecognizable as the tiny, peaceful village of those former times, for it is a busy, built-up area on the north-eastern outskirts of Leeds and is home to those who commute to the city. In 1948, however, the village was still very rustic.

One of the roads leading out of Scarcroft was known as Ling Lane. This was a narrow byway bordered by wide grass verges, clipped hawthorn hedges and gnarled old oak trees. It was a picturesque setting, and a short distance along the lane, leading from the village, was a pretty detached cottage. It was stone built and had beamed ceilings as it nestled behind a carefully trimmed hedge.

The house was Rose Cottage and was the home of a spinster lady called Ann Eleanor Barker. She was sixty-five years old and lived alone. She had lived with her aged mother at the cottage, but her mother had died just before the end of the Second World War, and so Ann continued to live alone at Rose Cottage. It was isolated, and although Ann was not a recluse, she did not invite many people into her home.

Lodged in the living-room of her small cottage there was a double-barrelled shotgun. Like so many countryfolk, the Barkers kept a gun for the destruction of vermin about their premises, and this one had probably belonged to Ann's father. It is not known whether Ann had ever used this weapon, but in any case it was kept high in the beams on the ceiling of her living-room, hardly the place to reach it during an emergency. Many countryfolk kept shotguns in this position.

Ann surely thought she had no need for a gun as a means of defence – but she was wrong.

She was considered a quiet person, one who kept herself to herself, for she did not have many close friends, although she was well known in and around the village. She had a small income but went out to work as a domestic help at some of the larger houses nearby; Scarcroft was then home to some wealthy and influential people, and these minor jobs helped her to meet people and earn a little extra cash.

She spent a quiet Christmas in 1948. Then, on the morning of Wednesday 29 December 1948, the village was shocked by the death of Ann Barker.

It was a chilly morning, but there had been no snow or rain, and life in the village was returning to normal after the Christmas break. At 8.30 a.m. the newspaper delivery lad called at Rose Cottage and left Ann's morning paper.

As was his practice, he pushed the folded paper into the handle of her front door above the sneck, where it remained on view; in doing so, he noticed nothing unusual.

About 10 a.m. that same day, a neighbour was passing and noticed the newspaper still in the door handle. She knocked on the door to see if Ann was ill or needed any help, but there was no reply. The neighbour thought it strange that there was no response, for Ann was always around the house, unless she was working. The lack of response to her knocking and shouting made her anxious, so she went for help and returned with a friend. They went to the rear door and were horrified to see that it had been forced open. They ventured into the cottage and found Ann lying dead on the floor, just inside the door. She had been subjected to some terrible physical injuries from which she had died. A blunt instrument of some kind had been used. The shotgun remained in its position in the rafters, having been used neither by the killer nor by the victim.

The village was within the West Riding of Yorkshire Police area, and detectives were quickly at the scene, where a full-scale murder investigation was launched. Teams of detectives commenced house-to-house enquiries around the village as they tried to establish a motive for Ann's death, and to discover whether or not anyone had been seen at the cottage.

These enquiries did produce one valuable piece of information. A villager had been in Ling Lane on the night prior to Ann's death; it was, at night especially, a very lonely place where few people walked, but the witness recalled having seen a strange man creeping along the lane. The time was around 10.30 that night, and the man was moving in a very odd manner which was described as a 'slouching gait'. The general impression was that the man was trying to be quiet and that he was doing his best to be unobserved. He was described as being about five feet seven inches tall, of medium build and wearing a cap, but the winter darkness prevented a more detailed description. At that time a light was burning at Ann's cottage – it was her paraffin lamp, and it showed through her curtains. It is thought that this may have attracted that man to her lonely home as he was passing.

Other than this sighting, there were no further clues to her death. The enquiries, which involved more than thirty detectives, were extended far beyond the boundaries of Scarcroft, and every man living in an area of some twenty-five square miles was interviewed and asked to account for his movements at the material time. But this produced nothing. The hunt for a murder weapon was equally meticulous. Every pond, wood, hedgeback and likely hiding-place was searched, and some of the deeper ponds around the village were even drained, but no weapon was ever found.

One factor that did immediately emerge, however, was the presence of a Polish workers' hostel in Wetherby Road, with several dozen residents. The police had to interview every one of them. This presented two major problems. The first was a matter of language. Whether or not any of them could speak English may never be known, but the sight of teams of English police officers wanting to ask them questions about their movements made them all claim to be unable to speak English. This meant fetching in interpreters. It is never easy to interview someone closely through an interpreter, and such interrogations are generally less than fully productive. During an interview of this kind, a police officer needs eye-to-eye contact with the witness during crucial questioning, but this was rendered useless in this case.

The language barrier was almost insurmountable. Nonetheless, the police were persistent. The Poles were confined to their mess room after their evening meal on the night of Wednesday 29 December for systematic interview, and this also enabled a search of their clothing to be made. The manner of Ann's violent death meant that the killer's clothing would surely be bloodstained.

As the examination of each man's clothing continued, all the efforts to abstract sensible responses from the Poles were unsuccessful. The interpreters, recruited from Leeds University, were unaccustomed to police procedures, and it proved virtually impossible to secure any kind of detailed responses. In spite of the difficulties, the enquiries continued until every Polish resident of that hostel had been interviewed. But it was to prove a valueless exercise. No useful information was obtained from them.

The second problem involved the Poles' clothing. The examination produced no evidence. According to one report, the police reckoned that, because the war had been over for only three years, these men would have few items of clothing. But they had many different suits and changes of clothing. Every man could boast four suits; one even had nine! They had several shirts too. In other words, a man could have thrown away an entire suit or change of bloodstained clothing without anyone missing it.

Searches of the hostel's likely places of concealment produced nothing, and there was no evidence of anyone's having burnt any clothing. The same applied to searches in the village and surrounding area. No remains of any discarded or bloodstained clothing were found.

A lot of effort went into the inquiries at the Polish workers' hostel, and requests for information were posted on noticeboards and places of public display in an effort to find witnesses. The notices were printed in Polish, German and English, and a reward of £1,000 was offered by a Sunday newspaper, but nothing further resulted.

The motive for Ann Barker's violent death was never established, and that remains one mystery. Another mystery is why such disturbing violence was used upon a quiet, defenceless woman who was approaching old age. She had no known enemies, no guilty secrets and no wealth of the kind that would attract such terrible treatment. Her appalling injuries did cause comparisons to be made with the Jack the Ripper cases in London and the murder of Kate Summerfield in Leeds some thirty-eight years earlier.

Another factor was the shotgun. Ann Barker had made no attempt to seize it and use it in her defence. Either her attacker was too swift for her to consider this action or else she knew him. Had he therefore entered without breaking in, later making it seem as if he had forced his way into the house in order to mislead the police into believing the killer was a stranger to her?

Was her killer an opportunist burglar who had been forced to kill to avoid capture or was he a local man who had killed to avoid identification? If so, why did he go into the house?

And would an opportunist burglar break into a house when a light was showing, as it was that night at Ann's quiet home?

The enquiries were intense, but the puzzle remains. Every police force in Britain was asked to trace the man with the slouching gait but he was never found.

No trace of the cottage remains, for it was later demolished.

So who killed Ann Eleanor Barker? And why?

Even today, someone, somewhere, might know the answer.

11   Two Village Mysteries

Fewston is a tiny village which is roughly midway between Harrogate and Skipton, just off the A59 road as it sweeps over Blubberhouses Moor. Before the boundary changes of 1974, it lay within the West Riding of Yorkshire, but it is now part of North Yorkshire.

Fewston lies in the Washburn Valley, which extends north from Wharfedale; the River Washburn rises on the moors above Pateley Bridge and flows through beautiful countryside before entering the Wharfe between Otley and Pool-in-Wharfedale. During its journey of little more than a dozen miles, it creates four reservoirs which have merged so well with the landscape that they appear to be natural lakes. First there is Thruscross Reservoir, then Fewston Reservoir, which almost adjoins Swinsty Reservoir, and finally Lindley Wood Reservoir.

The beautiful scenery which surrounds this area, and which is in a rough triangle based on Skipton, Harrogate and Otley, is part of the ancient Forest of Knaresborough and contains some of Yorkshire's most interesting scenery. One road which slices through the Washburn Valley is the B6551 from Otley to Summerbridge, and it was at a beauty spot known as Warren Point at Norwood Edge on Thursday 17 June 1982 that 29-year-old PC David Haigh of Harrogate was found murdered.

He had been shot through the head. His death was to set in motion Britain's largest manhunt, during which Sergeant David Winter of Malton and Mr George Luckett

159

of Girton near Lincoln were also murdered by the same roving gunman, a man called Barry Peter Prudom, also known as Barry Peter Edwards, who was born in Leeds in 1944. The ensuing manhunt occupied a total of seventeen days and included some of the wildest countryside in North Yorkshire and elsewhere. The killer was cornered near the tennis courts at Malton in Ryedale, where he shot and killed himself. There is a long account of this harrowing series of crimes in my companion volume, *Murders and Mysteries from the North York Moors*.

This inexplicable series of murders started almost within sight of Fewston, but it was not the first time that violent death had come to this village.

Fewston, being such a small community, is the last place one would expect murder and intrigue, although drama has come in other ways. It was once known as 'the moving village' because it sits on land which is regularly subjected to subsidence. It is thought that this is due to the construction of Swinsty Reservoir over which the village apparently presides. The sight of cracked houses, walls which leant at alarming angles and split buildings became something of a tourist attraction at the turn of the century. The present church, dating from 1697, overlooks the reservoir. The village's first two churches were both destroyed by fire, but the present building contains some fifteenth-century remnants.

One of Fewston's famous residents is buried within the churchyard. He is Edward Fairfax, a member of the famous Fairfax family as well as a poet and translator; he lived at New Hall and died in 1635. His work was enjoyed by two sovereigns – James I and Charles I – as well as by other literary figures. After his death, his former house was flooded and now lies beneath the reservoir. Rather surprising for such an intelligent man, he believed in witches and wrote on the topic of witchcraft. He thought his daughters were bewitched.

Today it is possible to visit one of the areas associated

with local witches. Nearby on Timble Gill Beck is a tiny stone packhorse bridge which crosses the stream near its entry into the River Washburn. This is a fairy bridge – or so the children believe – because it is so tiny, almost a model in fact. It honours a local rambler called Arthur Adamson, but it was here, years ago, that the Fewston Witches would meet for their secret ceremonies. I often wonder if Edward Fairfax came to observe them! There was a ghost too. It was here that a traveller was murdered by poachers years ago, and for centuries afterwards his ghost was said to haunt the area near this miniature bridge.

There is yet another oddity in Fewston churchyard. It was here that a gravestone marked the final resting-place of two men, father and son. The grave produces a mystery, because it records the death of Joseph Ridsdale on 29 February 1823 and his son on 30 February 1802. Neither of these dates existed.

Fewston is the setting for two more murders, one of which provides a mystery ...

Among the scattering of cottages and farms which formed this community before World War II, there was a fine building which served as the village shop. In 1938 the shopkeeper was Margaret Peel, aged thirty-seven. Her husband, Jesse Peel, who was thirty-nine, worked as a labourer for Leeds Corporation Water Works at the nearby Fewston and Swinsty reservoirs. By all accounts, the couple were happily married, and so far as anyone knew, there were no problems with the relationship.

At 7 a.m. one spring morning Jesse Peel left home to go to work as usual at the reservoirs. Just after 9.30 a.m. that same morning, the husband of the village schoolmistress saw Margaret Peel in her shop, alive and well.

Half an hour later a customer entered the tiny shop and was horrified to discover the body of Margaret Peel. She was lying in the shop and had been subjected to a ferocious beating which had killed her and left the shop and many of its contents covered with blood. This quiet village shopkeeper had been subjected to a most brutal and vicious attack.

The police were immediately called, and the investigation was led by Detective Chief Superintendent William Huddleston, a former military officer in the First World War and holder of the Military Cross. He acted with commendable speed: by noon that same day, more than 200 officers of the West Riding Constabulary were searching the surrounding countryside. Their task was twofold – they had to trace the killer, because surely he could not have travelled far, and they had also to trace any weapon he might have used and concealed. They had to pay close attention to the likelihood of discarded bloodstained clothing; this could have been hidden almost anywhere, including the reservoirs. So the search and the accompanying house-to-house enquiries sought anyone or anything that might have some links with the murder. Huddleston made use of the latest equipment in this search, for he took with him to Fewston a two-way radio network. This was the very first time that two-way radio had been used in Britain during a murder inquiry.

As the inquiry got underway, Jesse Peel was brought from work by the police and was accompanied to the scene. He was taken into his home, but there he acted in a rather strange manner: he did not go into that part of his house which formed the shop. When later he was asked why he had not gone into the shop, he explained that a policeman on duty had forbidden that. The officer had been told to let no one into the shop until the police had completed their examination of the scene and until the body had been removed to the mortuary. But he was then asked to enter, which he did.

At no time did he look upon his wife. He even stepped over her body without looking upon her so that he could check the till to see if any cash had been taken. Furthermore, he did not check a drawer in the house to see if his own money, a sum of £3, had been stolen.

Further suspicion was raised when Peel's clothing was examined, because bloodstains were found. There was blood on his waistcoat and, curiously, a bloodstain on his hat. Peel explained these by saying they had come from his hand which had been scratched by briars while he was clearing them from the banks of the reservoir.

Meanwhile the meticulous police search had found a possible murder weapon. A tyre lever was discovered in the reservoir, and the police felt it could have been used in the frenzied attack and thrown into the water.

One man, of course, had access to the water's edge, and his presence there would never arouse suspicion – Jesse Peel. Detective Chief Superintendent Huddleston came to the conclusion that Peel had killed his wife. He believed the fellow had come home from work after 9.30 a.m., killed his wife and returned to the reservoir, where he had disposed of the murder weapon. The bloodstains on his clothing gave support to Huddleston's suspicions; no other suspects had been seen in the village within the crucial time, and so Jesse Peel was arrested and charged with the murder of his wife.

At Peel's trial at Leeds Assizes, it was clear that the evidence against him was of the most circumstantial kind, with little or no real evidence which would prove his guilt. The small bloodstains helped to convince the jury of his innocence – had Peel killed his wife, the defence argued, his clothing would have been saturated with blood from her awful injuries. His clothing bore only tiny amounts, and furthermore no concealed clothing was ever found. So far as Peel was concerned, he had no known motive for murdering his wife – throughout their marriage the couple had been happy, and there was no suggestion of any traumas or upsets between them. At the end of a trial (which was criticized for ever taking place, due to the lack of firm evidence against Peel) he was acquitted. Members of the public in the gallery applauded the verdict, and Jesse

Peel returned to live at Fewston.

He was killed in 1942 in a traffic accident, and it was rumoured that he had confessed to the murder on his deathbed in Harrogate Hospital, but this is not true. In his examination of the case, Barry Shaw, in his book *Murderous Yorkshire* (Expressprint, Wakefield, 1980) recounts the evidence of a former police officer who was at Peel's side when he died. He affirmed that Jesse Peel did not confess to this killing. No other person has been found responsible for the murder of his wife, Margaret.

The reason for this brutal murder remains a mystery, for it appears to have been without a motive.

Fewston has links with yet another murder. Towards the end of May 1953 a 28-year-old car-dealer called Edward Watson, of Shadwell, near Leeds, returned home and told his wife that he had been frightened by the actions of another man. He said he had been to Harrogate to buy a car but told her that the seller, another car-dealer, had taken him into the woods and threatened to kill him. At the time he had not had with him the cash demanded by the other man. He was clearly upset by the experience.

Perhaps threats of this kind were not unusual within the shady world of second-hand-car dealing, but in this case Watson's worries did register with his wife. A week later he returned to Harrogate, this time with some cash to pay for a car he said he was going to purchase. The date was 2 June 1953, and in London there was a huge celebration, for it was the Coronation Day of Her Majesty Queen Elizabeth II.

When Watson failed to return home after that second trip to Harrogate, his wife became very concerned and recalled her husband's worries of a week earlier and his story of the threats in the wood. She went to the police and reported him missing. Leeds Police, knowing of Watson and his dealings, were not at all concerned, and in fact one of them suggested he might have gone to London to watch the festivities of the coronation.

Mrs Watson returned to her home in Ringwood Crescent, Shadwell, and waited. There was little else she could do. But she continued to worry and repeated her anxieties to the local police, and this time she did create some interest.

Detective Sergeant Wilby realized that her concern was genuine, and although his senior officers said he was wasting his time, he did begin his own enquiries. These led him to a car-dealer called Robert William Moore who lived in Harlow Avenue, Harrogate. In making background enquiries into Moore's recent behaviour, Wilby learned that he had recently bought a rifle and some ammunition, while someone else had observed him putting a spade into the boot of his car.

This provided sufficient motivation for Detective Sergeant Wilby to probe even deeper, and eventually he decided to interview Robert William Moore about his links with the missing Watson. He asked him about his recent movements and behaviour. When asked about the spade, for example, Moore said it was to dig his mother's garden, but Wilby learned that his mother had no garden, just a windowbox. Wilby then announced that the rifle would be required for ballistic examination, and this clearly affected Moore.

Moore was known to the police, and he had a peculiar habit of denying his involvement in any crime or offence by explaining exactly what he had done to commit it. When Detective Sergeant Wilby questioned him in depth about his links with the missing Watson, Moore asked, 'Do you think I've murdered him and buried him somewhere?'

Wilby now knew this was exactly what had happened and that he was faced with the difficult task of finding the body. Bearing in mind Mrs Watson's earlier story of her husband having been taken into a wood and threatened, the search was concentrated on the remote woodlands near Harrogate.

At this stage the enquiries were intensifying to such a degree that Moore realized that his crime would soon be discovered. He tried to commit suicide. Following this abortive attempt, he was arrested and taken into custody for further interviews. Eventually he admitted having shot Edward Watson and confessed that he had buried his body in woods near Fewston. He was then asked to take officers to the scene, and one night he showed them the grave. They began to dig among the trees in Primrose Cottage Plantation, Fewston, and quickly found the body of Edward Watson.

He had been shot at close range, and bullet holes were also found in a nearby tree.

Moore told the police it had all happened due to a deal which involved a faulty car. Moore had purchased a car at an auction and later found it had severe defects; he had traced its previous owner, who was Watson, and had tried to get some money back.

The first meeting between the pair of them, in the wood, resulted in the threats to Watson. On the second occasion Watson had agreed to meet Moore and had apparently agreed that he had been wrong to sell a car in such a dangerous condition. Watson had said he was prepared to make restitution, so Moore then said there was a cheap car for sale in Harrogate which might be of interest to Watson. Watson took £126 with him, a considerable sum at that time. It was a trap to lure him into a lonely place where he would be relieved of the cash. He was shot, robbed of the money and buried in that plantation. After the crime, Moore returned to his home in Harrogate to watch the coronation on television.

He was tried at Leeds Assizes and found guilty of murder, being sentenced to death on 25 November 1953, but he appealed against his sentence. The Home Secretary decided there were no grounds to interfere with the course of justice, and Robert William Moore was executed at Armley Gaol, Leeds, on 5 January 1954.

Surely one of the most baffling of crimes in the Yorkshire Dales is that which occurred at a remote hamlet called Bashall Eaves in 1934. It has featured in books and on televized documentary programmes but remains just as mysterious now as it was in March of that year. One odd aspect is that the victim actually saw his killer, then before he died he spoke to his sister about the incident, but in spite of this first-hand account of the shooting, the murderer has never been identified.

Bashall Eaves is perhaps the most distant of West Yorkshire's villages for it lies just within the county boundary where it adjoins Lancashire. The village and its people had, and still have, more affinity with the Lancashire towns of Clitheroe, Preston and Blackburn than with Yorkshire. Tucked under the southern edge of the Forest of Bowland, it is a tiny and isolated community on the road which crosses the beautiful fells of the Forest of Bowland between Great Milton and Lancaster via Sykes and Marshaw.

On Sunday 26 March 1934, at around 9.15 p.m., a local farmer called James Dawson was shot in the back while walking along a lane in the village, but the injury did not immediately kill him. In fact, according to his sister, he did not realize he had been shot and walked home in spite of the injury. Only later did he realize he had been wounded. He was then taken into hospital at Blackburn in Lancashire and died the following Thursday.

Somewhat strangely, the police were not told of the shooting until James Dawson died, thus losing a valuable four or five days of early and vital investigation. Another problem was that the head of West Yorkshire CID, Detective Chief Superintendent Wilfred Blacker, was working near York on another murder investigation, and he did not assume control of the Bashall Eaves killing until the Friday afternoon, although his deputy, Detective Superintendent Elliott, did commence the investigation as soon as the crime was reported. Nonetheless, delays of this kind are most unwelcome in any murder investigation, when a rapid response is so important. Once at the scene, however, Mr Blacker and his team did quickly set about the task of finding witnesses and searching for clues.

James Dawson was well known in the district, for he and his family farmed at the splendid Bashall Hall Farm set in rolling countryside. Among his interests was the breeding of game bantams, and in 1933 he had been a first-prize winner in a poultry show at Crystal Palace in London. It was his practice on a Sunday evening to walk to the Edisford Inn for a drink and a game of dominoes with his friends. On Sunday 26 March he walked to the pub as usual, had his drink and his game of dominoes and left at about 8.30 p.m. He walked towards his home at the farm, the final part of the journey being along a lane which led directly to his home.

As he walked up to the farmhouse, with some 200 yards to go before reaching home, he became aware of a man standing inside a farm gate. The gate was on the opposite side of the road to James. He walked past it, and as he was striding away, he heard a click. He felt something hit him in the back but thought it was local people playing a joke, perhaps lads throwing things such as mud or stones to annoy him. For this reason he ignored the incident and continued his journey home. When he arrived, everyone else was in bed; being farmers, they went to bed early and rose early next day.

James made himself some supper and went to bed. But then he felt his arm beginning to grow stiff, and when he undressed, he found blood on his clothes. Even then it seems he did not realize the extent or nature of his injury and only later told his sister about it. He related the odd incident in the lane and was taken to hospital in Blackburn for examination and treatment. He died four days later.

The police were told of the incident only upon the death of James Dawson, and thus the first mystery is created –

why were they not told of the shooting as soon as Dawson realized what had happened? He could have given a description of his assailant, but for some reason known only to himself, he did not report the attack.

When the bullet was recovered from his body, however, another mystery developed. The missile was made from steel and was unlike any of the known manufactured bullets; this one appeared to be home-made. The puzzle which now presented itself was what sort of weapon could have discharged it. Experts thought that a hand-gun was not involved, because the missile was too large for the known types of revolver or pistol, and in addition the accuracy of a hand-gun is notoriously poor over a great distance. The distance between the gate and the place where James received the wound was too great for an accurate aim when using a hand-gun, although an accidental or chance shooting could not be ruled out. It might have been an accidental or stray shot by someone experimenting with a home-made bullet.

However, the general consensus was that a .410 calibre shotgun could have projected such a missile. Many farmers and local people did possess .410 shotguns as well as the larger twelve-bores. Another theory was that the weapon used to fire the bullet might have been home-made. Poachers sometimes created guns out of bits and pieces of scrap metal, and such guns made little noise because they worked on a system similar to an air weapon: their missiles were projected by powerful air pressure rather than an explosive discharge; some experts said that the 'click' reported by James Dawson suggested the use of such a poacher's gun. A shotgun would have caused an explosive retort, not a click, and he would have recognized the sound. If his story of the shooting is true, had he been injured by a shotgun James would have surely made more of a fuss.

But it has never been satisfactorily established what kind of weapon did discharge the steel bullet which killed

James Dawson, and the actual weapon involved was never found.

As the police began their belated but meticulous house-to-house enquiries in the district, some witnesses did come forward. A youth from Clitheroe reported having seen a man wearing a smart, striped brown suit on the road between Bashall Eaves and Edisford Bridge. The man had made a remark about the farmer's being shot, adding that it was getting more like New York every day. Then he produced a revolver and showed it to the youth.

This encounter occurred on the Tuesday after the shooting, but before Dawson's death. The police were not, at that stage, involved, so the man could have been a local person who had heard rumours or exaggerated accounts of the shooting and who had decided to carry a revolver for self-protection out of fear of attack. The man in the brown suit has never been traced.

Other witnesses came forward to say they had seen the man standing inside the farm gate. It seems the killer knew Dawson's habits and was prepared to wait, even if it meant being noticed by passers-by. As the police enquiries continued, it became evident that at least three witnesses had seen the man at the farm gate. One was a motorist who had also noticed James Dawson walking home. Before Dawson had passed this way, a courting couple also saw the man and were not then suspicious because he made no effort to conceal himself. These were good witnesses because, in addition to having seen the man at the gate and noticed James Dawson, they had also observed three other people in the lane around the material times. It is possible that the other three also saw the man at the gate, thus creating the possibility that he was seen by at least seven people, one of whom was the murder victim.

In an effort to trace the unknown three people, the police asked for a message to be broadcast after the BBC news on Monday 26 March. It said that the police wished to interview anyone who had been in the vicinity at the time of the crime, especially the following: a broad-built man carrying a walking-stick; a man and woman with a farm dog; a man with an overcoat and trilby, with a woman in a great coat; a fairly tall man wearing a light-brown overcoat and trilby.

In such a small community, and within such a localized area as the farm lane, it is odd that so many people were around at the time of the shooting, and it would appear that most were from the district. But the village people were far from co-operative, and no further information was obtained.

There was a belief that Dawson had known his killer and that for some reason he was being protective. He might even have lied about the circumstances of his injury. Detective Chief Superintendent Blacker did not believe Dawson's own account of the shooting, albeit told through his sister, for he felt it was not possible for a man with such a serious wound in his back to walk the 200 yards to his home, make himself some supper and then go to bed before realizing he had been inflicted with a fatal wound.

Inevitably suspicion fell upon some local men, one story suggesting that Dawson had been caught by a jealous husband as he kissed the man's wife. Another rumour was that the wrong man had been shot, the intended victim being another farmer who had seduced a village girl who had later given birth to an illegitimate child.

The story is riddled with inconsistencies, Dawson's own account being one of them, and in spite of so many people having seen the man at the gate, he has never been identified. How is it that so many people were in the lane around the material time, and yet the man at the gate has never been identified?

When, in 1979, Yorkshire Television broadcast a documentary film about this murder, it was entitled *The Village That Would Not Talk*, and there is a fine account in Barry Shaw's book *Murderous Yorkshire* (Expressprint, Wakefield, 1980).

In spite of all the publicity and speculation, this murder has never been detected.

12   The Notorious Charles Peace

Charles Frederick Peace was a Yorkshireman and was the most notorious criminal in Britain during the Victorian era. At times bewilderingly charming, he could also be ruthlessly cruel. He was the killer of at least one policeman and one member of the public; he attempted to murder two other policemen and was guilty of a whole range of burglaries and housebreakings. There can be little doubt that he committed many serious crimes for which he was never prosecuted or even suspected.

There was another side to his complex character: this arch-villain and trickster was highly intelligent and very clever; he loved music and the arts, as well as being a skilled craftsman and was, somewhat surprisingly, a churchwarden. For many years, as a criminal who was hunted throughout the kingdom, he avoided capture by adopting clever disguises, false names, an abundance of charm and some bravado, and although he was feared by many, he was regarded by some as a kind of hero. The man was fascinating; his entire life and behaviour were a puzzle which criminologists have constantly found of deep interest.

Charles Peace was born in Angel Court, Sheffield, in May 1832 and, although little is known of his formative years, it is known that he was a young ruffian who frightened his contemporaries. He organized small peepshows for his friends, using trained cats and other popular amusements of the period.

Upon leaving school, he emulated his father and went to work in a steel mill but suffered injuries to a leg which affected him throughout his later life. When his father died, it is claimed that young Peace tied his mother to her chair in an attempt to impose his dominance upon the household. There is every probability that he started his criminal career when he was a child, but it assumed greater importance after his father's death.

Because young Peace and his mother were always short of funds, Charlie, as he was known, turned to crime as a means of raising money. His first known burglary was upon a house in Mount View, Sheffield, where he stole a pair of duelling pistols. After he sold one, he was captured and prosecuted for this crime, being sentenced to a month in gaol.

Upon his release, he committed more burglaries around Sheffield, always seeking high-quality goods and money, and he did so by climbing the porticoes of the large houses he raided. This became recognized as his MO (*modus operandi*), and through it the police knew the raids were the work of one criminal. In time, Charlie Peace was arrested and sentenced to four years' penal servitude.

After this sentence, it seems he either ceased his criminal activities or was never caught, for he returned to work at the steel mill and earned some honest extra cash by becoming an entertainer. He played the violin and sang to his own accompaniment, billing himself as 'The Modern Paganini' or 'The Great Ethiopian Musician'. In the latter case, he adopted a disguise which he was later to use in his criminal activities. He coloured his skin with walnut juice, and it seems this was highly effective, many believing he did come from overseas.

He even composed a highly popular song which was sung throughout the country and in addition worked as a joiner and picture-framer to try to raise money. Whether his craftsmanship was of a high quality is not known.

When Peace was twenty-seven years old, he married.

His bride was a widow, Mrs Hannah Ward, who had a son. In the year of his marriage, 1859, he raided a house across the Pennines in Lancashire and was caught. He said his name was George Parker from Nottingham and that he also used the name Alexander Mann. He was sentenced to six years' penal servitude.

While in prison, he became the father of a son, but the child was born dead; he was named John Charles Peace. Then, in June 1864, Charlie was released before the end of his sentence. He returned to Sheffield and became a father for the second time: he had a daughter called Jane Ann.

His prison terms did not deter him from burgling, for he continued to raid expensive houses in the area, now armed with pistols. It was claimed that Charles Peace was always armed during his raids on expensive properties and that on one occasion a pistol accidentally discharged itself. It shot off two of Charlie's fingers, thus deforming his left hand in a most distinctive way. He was caught again and served yet another term of imprisonment, coming out in August 1872. Now he tried to reform himself, setting up in business as a picture-framer in Sheffield. This business was a success, and in 1875 he was able to move his family to a better house.

Charlie was now middle-aged. He was forty-three years old, five feet three inches tall, with a balding head, an ugly bearded face described as monkey-like, slurred speech, a deformed hand, an injured leg which gave him a peculiar wide-legged gait, and an evil smell which constantly surrounded him. He was not a handsome man by any standards; in fact, he was downright ugly. In addition, his behaviour had become bizarre – he would froth at the mouth when he became angry, sometimes shaking uncontrollably, and he was known to beat his wife without mercy when his ungovernable temper got out of hand. In short, Charles Peace was anything but an attractive man. Many men of his age and appearance would have settled into a quiet, domestic life, especially when running such a successful business, but Charles Peace was unsettled and needed excitement; he was also ambitious to earn more money and, being a natural criminal, this period marked the true beginning of a law-breaking career which has placed his name firmly in the annals of British crime.

At this time Charlie's new home was next door to that of a man called Arthur Dyson and his family. Arthur was a law-abiding citizen who worked as a civil engineer. He had an attractive wife, Katherine, twenty years younger than himself, and they had a six-year-old son. Peace developed a passion for Katherine. He always regarded himself as a charmer and started to visit his neighbour. Sometimes he would eavesdrop upon the Dysons' conversations or peer through their windows. He became a gross nuisance, tripping Arthur in the street, and eventually Arthur Dyson warned him off. Charlie retorted that he would blow out Dyson's brains, and continued to be a nuisance, especially through his unwanted attention to Katherine.

Dyson, probably unaware that Peace carried a gun, then took legal proceedings against him, to stop the nuisance. Peace appeared to resolve the problem by moving his home to Hull, but he asked an old friend to keep him informed of events surrounding Katherine Dyson, for he remained obsessed by her.

In October 1876 Peace heard that the Dysons were moving house, and so he hurried to watch their departure. As the van moved off with their belongings, he followed it to Banner Cross Terrace, the Dysons' new home, and there he accosted Katherine. He said he would follow her wherever she went. After this odd meeting, he returned to Hull, violently assaulted his wife, Hannah and threw her and his family out of the family home. Then he closed down the house and never went back. Thus he began his life as a wandering criminal.

It is known that he travelled the country committing

burglary, some of his excursions taking him into Lancashire. There a policeman, PC Nicholas Cock, was murdered at Whalley Range near Manchester, but Charles Peace was never suspected of this. Indeed, two brothers, John and William Habron, were arrested and brought to trial for the crime. On 28 November 1876 Peace told his friends that he was going to visit Manchester Assizes to listen to a case which intrigued him. There he heard the jury find John Habron not guilty of murdering PC Cock but declare William Habron guilty. He was sentenced to death.

Charlie then took a train to Sheffield and for some odd reason called on a vicar, the Revd E. Newman. He told the astonished vicar that he had been having an affaire with Katherine Dyson and claimed that Arthur Dyson's actions, in earlier taking legal process against him, had broken up his own happy family at Hull.

Then Peace went to Banner Close Terrace and was in time to see Katherine emerge from her home and cross to an outside toilet. When she came out, she was confronted by Charles Peace, who was holding a revolver. She screamed and leapt back into the toilet, locking the stout door as she continued to scream and call for help. The commotion alerted Arthur, who rushed out to find a man running away. Arthur gave chase, but the man halted and fired; the first shot missed but Arthur continued his pursuit, and the second shot hit him in the head. It was a fatal wound.

The neighbours had been aroused by the screams and shots, but as Arthur lay dying in his wife's arms, Charles Peace escaped into the darkness. Later he calmly called on his brother, who lived in Sheffield, and finally caught a train back to Hull. His wife, Hannah, had opened some refreshment rooms in Hull, and so he went there and demanded food and accommodation.

But the alert had been raised and Charles Peace was being hunted for the murder of Arthur Dyson. As Charlie settled down at Hull, two policemen called at the refreshment rooms and asked Hannah if he was at home; they could not see him, but he heard their request and was quick enough to escape onto the roof via an upstairs window and so avoided capture.

But when 'Wanted' posters appeared in Hull next day, naming Charles Frederick Peace as the murderer of Arthur Dyson and bearing a fairly good description of the suspect, Charlie knew it was time to flee. There was a reward of £100 for information leading to his arrest and so he shaved off his beard, acquired a pair of heavy spectacles and dyed his hair. He changed his mode of dressing too and bought new clothes, then made a curious false arm of leather and wood which encased and concealed his deformed hand. He fled from Hull, taking with him some of the fruits of his burglaries in and around the East Riding of Yorkshire.

He made his way to Nottingham, where he found a relation who was willing to provide him with shelter, and he made friends with a Mrs Susan Bailey who called herself Mrs Thompson. Peace's creative abilities and business acumen surfaced again, and he established a business making marking inks for industry. While Mrs Thompson helped with the business, he went burgling good houses but also specialized in warehouse raids. Through these, he acquired a mass of high-quality silk goods, but the police identified the villain responsible, and so Charlie fled from Nottingham, taking Mrs Thompson with him. Rumours suggested they had crossed to the Continent, but in fact he remained in the Midlands and north of England.

One account suggests that he cheekily returned to Hull, where he and Mrs Thompson lodged with a police sergeant and his family: the sergeant even praised his lodger's skill with the artificial hand, the lodger in return demonstrating his prowess with a fork at meal times. While in Hull, Peace took his mistress to meet his wife,

Hannah! But the pressure in Yorkshire was too much, and Charlie fled south to London, where he bought two houses – one for Hannah and his children, the other for Mrs Thompson, alias Sue or Felicity Bailey. Like her lover, she was adept at making use of false names.

In London Peace lived in Lambeth and called himself John Ward as he established his credibility as a dealer in musical instruments. He was, in fact, stealing high-quality violins and other stringed instruments, for he was, in spite of his new respectability, a busy and successful burglar. He always worked alone, and he went about in a good-quality suit in the belief that no one would suspect such a smart businessman. At one time the spate of burglaries and housebreakings caused the police to believe that gangs of burglars were responsible.

Then, having exhausted suitable victims in Lambeth, Peace moved to Greenwich, where he was able to buy a fine, large house and became known as a gentleman of independent means. Soon Greenwich was experiencing a massive crime wave. Numerous burglaries were committed at the homes of important residents, from which jewels, silverware and high-quality furnishings were stolen. Peace next moved to an even larger house in Peckham and called himself Johnson.

His new house was exquisitely filled with beautiful furnishings. The drawing-room contained a fine walnut suite, then worth up to 60 guineas. A Turkey carpet lay on the floor; many of the walls had valuable mirrors; there was a bijou piano and an inlaid Spanish guitar, a fine collection of valuable violins and all the trappings of a gentleman of wealth and distinction. Indeed, when this house became too full of stolen goods, Peace bought or rented others in the area. He placed a respectable woman in charge of each one and filled them all with valuable goods. When he wanted money, he would send the ladies out to sell or pawn the items, making sure they operated at a good distance from the scene of the original thefts. Thus he persuaded innocent people to assist him in his crimes.

But, like so many criminals, Charlie Peace was greedy: he could not stop his passion for collecting fine objects through crime. By now some two years had passed since he had killed Arthur Dyson, and he had almost forgotten that he was still wanted for that murder; he thought that no one would catch him now, for he was still living under false names.

His burglary activities were his real profession, and he equipped himself with a range of equipment, most of it made and invented by himself. He had a sharp knife with a wooden handle, his false arm, various devices for picking locks, a gimlet for boring into the frames of windows to facilitate entry, a portable vice to act as a third hand, a hand-held bit for boring into difficult places and a gouge for removing putty. His other instruments of burglary included dark glasses, and one of his proudest possessions was a collapsible ladder he had made from wood; he used this for climbing up to windows and other points of entry. Upon his eventual conviction, these items were placed in Scotland Yard's Black Museum.

Not yet satisfied with his treasury of ill-gotten gains, Charles Peace went out to commit yet another burglary. The date was 17 November 1878.

In the early hours of the day, he went to 2 St John's Park, Blackheath in London, knowing it would yield rich pickings. Peace was selective; he was a raider only of upper-class homes. He effected a swift entry into the empty premises, but a patrolling constable, PC Edward Robinson, noticed a suspicious light on the ground floor and, instead of tackling the intruder alone, called for assistance.

When the second constable arrived, they made their plans to cover the exits. One of them rang the door bell. The light went out. They waited and then, as anticipated, a dark figure crept out of the house through the drawing-room window, and PC Robinson called out a challenge. The man replied that, if the officers came forward, he would shoot. In spite of this, they moved in and Peace fired five shots at them. PC Robinson was badly wounded but managed to arrest his assailant, who struggled to the extent of throwing the officer to the ground. There Peace tried to stab him, but he was soon overpowered and arrested. He was taken to the police station.

The skin of the captured little man was so dark that the police thought they had arrested a foreigner or a half-caste. He refused to give any details of himself, but when he was searched, it was found he had a revolver strapped to his wrist; it was brand new and manufactured in America. The police now realized they had a hardened criminal and, when pressed for a name and address, he said he was a half-caste called John Ward who had just come from America. He looked to be sixty years of age, although he was only forty-six.

The police did not allow him bail. He was remanded in custody as they continued their careful enquiries. These led to the home of a Mr Johnson, also known as John Ward; this was a fine house in one of the smartest areas of Peckham, the home of a churchwarden and hardly the sort of house to be occupied by a burglar and would-be killer.

A search of the house soon revealed the truth. Stolen goods, such as jewellery, furnishings, gold and silver plate and other valuables, were discovered in the house, as well as pawn tickets and other evidence of 'Ward's' one-man crime wave. He was charged with burglary and with having attempted to murder PC Robinson, and was sent for trial at the Old Bailey.

Peace – as 'Ward' – was found guilty and sentenced to penal servitude for the rest of his natural life; everyone involved thought he was some sixty years old and that such a sentence might not be a long one! He was sent to
. Pentonville Prison.

But hell hath no fury like a woman spurned, and Peace had made one fatal error in his carefully plotted criminal life. He had allowed Sue Bailey, alias Felicity Bailey, alias Mrs Thompson, to learn his secrets. It seems that she felt she had been tricked by her lover. She began to think she had been used by him, that she meant nothing to him and that he was only making a convenience of her. Apart from that, she was also greedy and needed money.

Under her name of Bailey, she wrote to the authorities to claim the £100 reward still outstanding for information leading to the arrest of Charles Peace for the murder of Arthur Dyson in Sheffield. Upon receipt of her letter, the police took immediate action. A detective who knew Peace was sent to Pentonville to examine the prisoner and immediately identified him as the master criminal who was still wanted for the murder of Arthur Dyson on 22 November 1876.

Peace was therefore taken by train to Sheffield police station, from which he would eventually stand trial at Leeds Assizes. It was during this journey that he attempted a dramatic escape which helped to place his name before the public. As the train sped north at express speed, he suddenly leapt free of his escort and dived out of the carriage window. This occurred between Shireoaks and Kiveton Park on the line between Worksop and Sheffield. Thick snow lay on the ground at the time and undoubtedly helped to save Charlie Peace from death. As he fell, he broke a leg and suffered other, lesser injuries. As he tried to crawl to freedom, the train was halted, a search was made and he was caught.

Some claimed that this was really a suicide attempt that failed, Peace knowing that he would be sentenced to death, while others maintained that the leap was in character, that Peace was trying yet another desperate dash for freedom.

It was some weeks before he was fit enough to stand trial, and he appeared at Leeds Assizes on 4 February 1879 charged with the murder of Arthur Dyson. He looked like an aged wreck of a man. The unhappy Katherine Dyson had no difficulty identifying Peace as the man who had pestered her and then killed her husband, and even though Peace tried to pass the blame to Mrs Dyson, the jury found him guilty. They reached their verdict in just over ten minutes.

Charles Peace was sentenced to death; his appeals for clemency were rejected and he was lodged in Armley Gaol at Leeds to await his sentence. The execution was scheduled to take place on 25 February 1879.

While in Armley, he asked to speak to the governor, to whose astonishment Peace calmly admitted having killed PC Cock in Manchester some three years earlier. He reminded the governor that two men had been tried for that crime, one of whom had been found guilty. Peace said the man was totally innocent. Fortunately the Home Secretary had commuted William Habron's sentence to one of life imprisonment. At the time of this news, he was serving his sentence by breaking rocks in a quarry, and so he lived to enjoy his freedom. He was given a free pardon and £800 compensation.

Having cleared his conscience of this injustice, Charles Peace prepared himself for death. Before his appointment with William Marwood, his executioner, he prayed with his wife and daughter and chatted with the reporters who had assembled.

His execution was to be in private, the last public executions at Armley being those of Joseph Myers and James Sargisson, both on 10 September 1864, fifteen years before the turn of Charles Peace.

On the morning of his execution he ate a hearty breakfast and was then taken to the scaffold. He had tried to delay the execution for an hour by saying he was expecting a vital letter, but the under-sheriff, Mr W. Gray, refused to amend the procedures.

At 8 a.m. on 25 February 1879, therefore, Charles

Frederick Peace was executed by hanging. His body was buried within the precincts of Armley Gaol.

But for years afterwards there were stories about him. Some said he had once met Marwood on a train journey and had asked the executioner to grease the rope, should they ever meet one another professionally. On another train journey, he had discussed with two detectives the best way of catching the notorious criminal Charles Peace. And it was said that moments before his death he had complained that the halter was too tight.

There is no doubt that Peace committed countless burglaries and thefts for which he was never charged or prosecuted, and it is also claimed that he committed many other murders during his final rampage of crime. But he admitted only to the murder of PC Cock. One account, by a man who knew him and who talked with him in the death cell, says that Peace did not die a penitent man. He was defiant until the last moment.

So was the notorious Charles Peace guilty of other murders?

We shall never know.

Index

Poisonings, 92–5, 97
Pontefract, 45, 46
Poole-in-Wharfedale, 159
Portland cement, 149
Pot-holing, 101 et seq.
Prehistoric finds, 105
Preston, 167
Prince, Augustin le, 148
Prudom, Barry Peter, 160
Public Records Office, 47
Puck, 42
Pye, Emily, 141 et seq.

Racehorses, 58
Ramsgill, 70
Rawcliffe, 24
Recusants, 65
Reeth, 20, 124
Reformation, 59, 64, 81, 119
Reservoirs
    Cow Green, 121
    Bilberry, 118
    Fewston, 159, 161
    Leighton, 18
    Lindley Wood, 154
    Scar House, 122
    Swinsty, 159–61
    Thruscross, 159
Ribblesdale, 56, 57
Richard I, 43
Richard III, 58
Richmond, 7, 23, 63
Ripley Castle, 70
Ripon, 7, 46, 49, 70, 71, 76
Rippers
    Jack the Ripper, 146–7
    Leeds Rippers, 146 et seq.
    Yorkshire Ripper, 147
Rivers
    Aire, 24
    Burn, 19
    Calder, 39, 52
    Don, 119
    Humber, 85
    Nidd, 15, 79, 102
    Ouse, 85
    Skell, 49
    Swale, 10, 20, 85, 128, 131, 132

Tees, 70, 118, 119, 120
Tutt, 12
Ure, 10, 13, 49, 59
Washburn, 159
Wharfe, 28, 34
Robert, St (cave), 79, 80, 81, 83
Robin de Kyme, 47
Robin Fitz-Ooth, 45
Robin Goodfellow, 42
Robin Hood's Bay, 42, 48
Robin Hood's Day, 50
Robin Hood's grave, 53–4
Roecliffe, 11
Robinson, PC Edward, 180
Robinson Pot, 101
Romanby, 127 et seq.
Romans, 9, 10, 11, 12, 13, 39, 58,
    104, 105, 153
Rossington, 24
Rumbald, 9
Rumbald's Moor, 10
Ryedale, 160

Saint
    Alkelda, 56 et seq.
    Alkelda's Well, 57, 62
    Arild, 61
    Cedd, 60
    Cuthbert, 13, 60
    Hilda, 60, 138
    Margaret Clitherow, 64 et seq.
    Mary, 57
    Mary's Abbey, 71
    Robert's Cave, 79, 80, 81, 83
Scarborough, 48, 95, 97, 127
Scarcroft, 153 et seq.
Scar House Reservoir, 122
Scotland, King of, 124
Scotland Yard, 143, 180
Scotsmen, 105, 122, 123
Scotten, 124
Settle, 104, 105
Shadwell, 164
Shakespeare, William, 86, 124, 127
Sheard, Emma, 112 et seq.
Sherwood Forest, 38, 46, 55
Shipton, Mother, 16, 70
Sheffield, 41, 45, 47, 173, 177, 182